Newfoundland and Labrador Outstanding Outhouse Reader

Newfoundland and Labrador Outstanding Outhouse Reader

VERNON OICKLE

MacIntyre Purcell Publishing Inc

Copyright 2016 Vernon Oickle

All rights reserved. No part of this book covered by the copyrights hereon may be reproduced or used in any form or by any means – graphic, electronic, or mechanical – without the prior written permission of the publisher. Any request for photocopying, recording, taping, or information storage and retrieval systems of any part of this book shall be directed in writing to the Canadian Reprography Collective, 379 Adelaide Street, West, Suite M1, Toronto, Ontario, M5V 1S5.

MacIntyre Purcell Publishing Inc.
194 Hospital Rd.
Lunenburg, Nova Scotia
B0J 2C0
(902) 640-3350

www.macintyrepurcell.com
info@macintyrepurcell.com

Printed and bound in Canada by Marquis.

Cover Art: Kevin O'Reilly

Library and Archives Canada Cataloguing in Publication

Oickle, Vernon, 1961-, author   Newfoundland and Labrador outstanding outhouse reader / Vernon Oickle.

ISBN 978-1-77276-012-5 (paperback)

      1. Newfoundland and Labrador--Miscellanea.   2. Newfoundland and Labrador--Humor. I. Title.

FC2161.6.O33 2016   971.8002   C2016-902197-1

MacIntyre Purcell Publishing Inc. would like to acknowledge the financial support of the Government of Canada and the Nova Scotia Department of Tourism, Culture and Heritage.

Funded by the Government of Canada

INTRODUCTION

The big rock in the middle of the Atlantic is pretty unique at times, even compared to the rest of Canada. It's also a place of fascinating history and culture, being one of the oldest colonized settlements in North America.

As I undertook this project, I did so with a great deal of excitement and enthusiasm. While I don't live in Newfoundland and Labrador, I have visited this uniquely wonderful province several times. To be able to research and write about such an exquisite place was a tremendous opportunity and a rewarding experience for me as it gave me new insight into this place that is, for the most part, a world unto itself.

Beyond its rich culture and history, the one thing that has impressed me most about Newfoundland and Labrador is the fantastic people who live there. I've known some wonderful people who come from the Island and I can say without hesitation that they are among the most generous, thoughtful and kind people you will find anywhere.

I have always believed that a place is just a place filled with rocks, natural vegetation, waterways and the structures we build, but it is the people that truly give any place its charm and character. Indeed, there is no better example of that than the Province of Newfoundland and Labrador.

This book represents a collection of interesting information, intriguing stories and fascinating facts about Canada's youngest province. It is meant to inform and enlighten, but more importantly it is meant to entertain. In terms of saying thank you, I should point out this book would not be possible without the generous support and encouragement of publisher John MacIntyre at MacIntyre Purcell Publishing Inc. Somehow John, saying thanks just does not seem like enough!

As well, I must send a special note of thanks to designer Alex Hickey, who always does such a wonderful. The book looks great.

It is my hope that you learn as much about this wonderful place as I have.

— Vernon Oickle

CONTENTS

INTRODUCTION..5

ABOUT NEWFOUNDLAND AND LABRADOR......................9
   THE PEOPLE • CLIMATE • HISTORY • LAND AND WATER • RESOURCES/INDUSTRY • PROVINCIAL SYMBOLS • PROVINCIAL FLAG • THE SEA PARROT • IN COD WE TRUST

CULTURE AND COMMUNICATION...........................19
   A NEWFOUNDLAND SCOFF • NEWFOUNDLAND SPECIALTIES • HISTORY WAS MADE WITH THREE CLICKS • THE PRINTED WORD ON THE AIR • IT'S FOR YOU • AT THE MOVIES • LOVE AND MARRIAGE • IT'S OFF TO SCHOOL WE GO • AFTER SCHOOL ACTIVITY • HALF AN HOUR LATER IN NEWFOUNDLAND

DISASTERS..35
   THE CRASH OF ARROW AIR FLIGHT 1285 • THE BELL ISLAND BOOM • ST. JOHN'S KNIGHTS OF COLUMBUS HALL FIRE • SINKING OF THE *OCEAN RANGER* • SINKING OF *TITANIC* • THE NEWFOUNDLAND TSUNAMI • THE 1914 SEALING DISASTER

FAMOUS NEWFOUNDLANDERS AND LABRADORIANS..........55
   LIGHTS. CAMERAS. ACTION!

FASCINATING FACTS...73
   ONE FOR THE RECORD BOOKS • OVER THE LIPS … • SCREECH-IN • LADIES FIRST • FLYING INTO THE HISTORY BOOKS • GONE TO THE DOGS • A RARE BREED, INDEED

GEOGRAPHY/WEATHER......................................87
   THE LAY OF THE LAND • THE FURTHEST EAST YOU CAN GO • THE LEWIS HILLS • THE LONG RANGE MOUNTAINS • LET IT SNOW, LET IT SNOW, LET IT SNOW • ONE FOR THE RECORD BOOKS • THE ANSWER IS BLOWING IN THE WIND • OUTPORT REPORT • RAWLINS CROSS • ROUND OR FLAT?

HISTORICALLY SPEAKING...................................97
   THE BEOTHUK • THE INUIT OF LABRADOR • THE INNU MI'KMAQ • THE VIKINGS ARRIVE 500 YEARS BEFORE COLUMBUS • JOHN CABOT DISCOVERS NEWFOUNDLAND • AN HISTORIC SITE • FIRST ENGLISH BURIAL GROUNDS • THE GOLDEN AGE OF PIRATES • THE OLDEST ON THE CONTINENT • REACH FOR THE SKY • LET THERE BE LIGHT • UNESCO SITES • FIRST WORLD WAR • UNDER ATTACK

INVENTIONS 133
    JUST A GAS

LAW AND ORDER 135
    LEGAL NOTES • SHOOT TO KILL • BREAKING THE BANK
    HANG'EM HIGH • SPEAKING OF HANGING • FOR THE RECORD
    IN THE LINE OF DUTY • WRONGLY CONVICTED • THE
    MOUNT CASHEL SCANDAL • THE ROYAL NEWFOUNDLAND
    CONSTABULARY • THE FIRST OF HER KIND

LEGENDS, GHOSTS AND SUPERSTITIONS 147
    SHEILA'S BRUSH • THE OLD HAG OF NEWFOUNDLAND •
    MUMMERING • THE VIKING GHOST SHIP • THE HAG OF BELL
    ISLAND • VICTORIA STREET VISITORS • NEWFOUNDLAND'S
    OWN LOCH NESS MONSTER • DEVIL'S HAND • THE PIRATE
    TREASURE OF TORBAY • THE MYSTERY OF THE RESOLVEN
    • THE KNOCKING OF FORAN'S HOTEL • THE CRY •
    SUPERSTITIONS • IT IS GOOD LUCK TO … • SIGNS OF DEATH •
    OFF TO SEA

POLITICS 159
    THE BIRTH OF A PROVINCE • PREMIERS OF NEWFOUNDLAND
    AND LABRADOR SINCE JOINING CONFEDERATION • THE LITTLE
    MAN FROM GAMBO

TRANSPORTATION 165
    PLANES, TRAINS AND AUTOMOBILES

GLOSSARY OF NAMES 171

FIVE FAST FACTS

1 Newfoundland has its own time zone, although Labrador does not. Newfoundland is 30 minutes ahead of Atlantic Time.

2 Archaeologists working in Cupids discovered the earliest known English cemetery in Canada and it is believed to be more than 400 years old.

3 An estimated 99 percent of the world's population of critically endangered Boreal Felt Lichen is found on the Island of Newfoundland.

4 The only known case of German's landing in North America during the Second World War was in Newfoundland. On October 22, 1943, German submarine U-537 landed on Martin Bay in the north of Labrador and set up a remote weather station. It was forgotten and wasn't visited again until 1981.

5 There are no crickets, snakes, raccoons, skunks, deer, porcupine or groundhogs on the Island.

Moss and lichen close-up in Nordic landscape.

ABOUT NEWFOUNDLAND AND LABRADOR

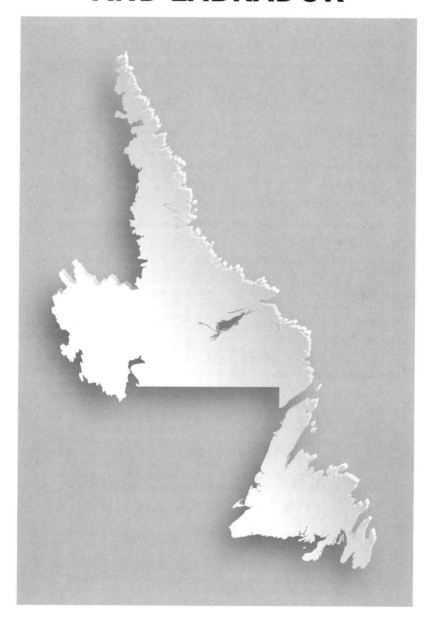

THE PEOPLE

- 528,448 people live in Newfoundland and Labrador based on a 2016 estimate.
- Most of the population lives on the Island of Newfoundland.
- About 60 percent of the people live in towns and cities.
- Early settlers mainly came from England, Ireland and Scotland.
- About 96 percent are British and Irish, and about two percent are of French descent.
- Aboriginal ancestry includes Mi'kmaq, Inuit, Innu and Métis.

CLIMATE

- In northern Labrador, the climate is subarctic.
- The Atlantic Ocean affects the climate.
- Summers are cool and winters are long.
- There are many storms, fog, strong winds, heavy precipitation and cold temperatures.
- Newfoundland experiences more fog than any of the other Atlantic Provinces.

HISTORY

- The first people of Newfoundland were the Beothuk (now extinct) who hunted caribou and fished.
- For thousands of years, ancestors of the Inuit hunted seal and polar bears along the Labrador coast.
- Vikings (Norsemen) were the first to visit Newfoundland and Labrador.
- Five hundred years later (in 1497), the explorer John Cabot arrived. He claimed the "new found isle" for the King of England.
- Fishermen from France, England, Spain and Portugal fished in the waters of the Grand Banks.
- English, Irish and Scottish settlers built small villages along the coast.
- In 1949, Newfoundland became Canada's tenth province.

LAND AND WATER

- There are many bays and deep fiords along the coastlines.
- Thousands of small islands are also included.
- Labrador is larger and is bordered by Quebec. The North Atlantic Ocean is to the east.
- The Island of Newfoundland is surrounded by the Gulf of St. Lawrence and the Atlantic Ocean.
- Thick forests and many rivers and lakes cover much of the Island and south and central Labrador.
- Torngat Mountains, in Labrador, are the most spectacular mountains east of the Rockies.
- Gros Morne National Park (west coast of Newfoundland) has mountains, forests, lakes and sand dunes.
- Terra Nova National Park (east coast of Newfoundland) consists of rocky cliffs, rolling hills, forests, lakes and ponds.
- The Continental Shelf, off the coast, includes shallow areas (banks) and deeper areas (troughs and channels).
- The Grand Banks are a shallow part of the Continental Shelf (less than 50 metres deep) that lie off the coast of Newfoundland.

RESOURCES/INDUSTRY

- Main exports are oil, fish products, newsprint, iron ore and electricity.
- Newfoundland and Labrador are part of the Canadian Shield.
- Iron ore is produced in Labrador. (Steel is made from iron ore.)
- Oil and gas are found under the Grand Banks.
- Churchill Falls in Labrador is the second largest underground hydroelectric power plant in the world.
- Fishermen catch cod, herring, Atlantic salmon, flounder, turbot, halibut, tuna and haddock.
- Lobster, scallops, shrimp, and crab are also caught.
- Overfishing caused a severe decline of fish in the Grand Banks.
- Fish processing is an important industry.
- Forests (mostly coniferous trees) cover one third of Newfoundland.
- Summers are cool and the growing season is short.

More than 100 years ago, Queen Victoria chose the pitcher plant to be engraved on a newly minted Newfoundland penny. In 1954 the Newfoundland cabinet designated this interesting plant as the official flower of the province. The pitcher plant gets its nourishment from insects that are trapped and drown in a pool of water at the base of its tubular leaves. These plants, with their wine and green flowers, are found on bogs and marshes around the province.

PROVINCIAL SYMBOLS

- The provincial capital is the City of St. John's. It is the largest city in the province and it is also the oldest city in North America.
- Provincial flower — Pitcher Plant.
- Provincial tree — Black Spruce.
- Provincial bird — Atlantic Puffin.
- Provincial motto — "Seek ye first the Kingdom of God."
- Provincial animal — Caribou (unofficial).

PROVINCIAL FLAG

Newfoundland and Labrador Provincial Flag.

- The flag of Newfoundland and Labrador was introduced in 1980, and was designed by Newfoundland artist Christopher Pratt. The design was approved by the House of Assembly of the Province of Newfoundland and Labrador on May 28, 1980. It was flown for the first time on Discovery Day, June 24, 1980.

The design was chosen due to its broad symbolism. The blue colour represents the sea, the white colour represents snow and ice of winter, the red colour represents the effort and struggle of Newfoundlanders and Labradorians, and the gold colour symbolizes the confidence Newfoundlanders and Labradorians have in themselves and for the future.

The blue triangles are meant as a tribute to the Union Jack, and stand for the British heritage of Newfoundland and Labrador. The two red triangles are meant to represent the two areas of the province — the mainland and the Island. The gold arrow, according to Pratt, points towards a brighter future, the arrow becomes a sword, honouring the sacrifices of Newfoundlanders in military service when the flag is draped as a vertical banner. The red triangles and the gold arrow form a trident, symbolizing the province's dependence on its fisheries and the resources of the sea.

THE SEA PARROT

Puffin (Fratercula arctica) in green grassy vegetation near nesting burrow in breeding colony on an island.

The Atlantic puffin is instantly recognizable by its white face and large and colourful orange, yellow and blue-grey bill in which, during breeding season, it carries a dozen or more capelin back to its single chick. It is known locally as a "sea parrot" or "hatchet-face" for its distinctive looks.

Newfoundland and Labrador is home to North America's three largest puffin breeding colonies. With roughly 260,000 pairs, the top nesting location is Witless Bay

Islands while Baccalieu Island and Gannet Islands in Labrador rank second and third on that list.

Puffins breed in burrows or crevices in rocky cliffs. They dive from the water's surface after food, using their short wings to go as deep as 60m in pursuit of prey. They don't take to the air as easily, however — scrambling frantically along the surface until airborne, flapping their wings at hundreds of beats per minutes in flight and often crash landing when out of danger.

IN COD WE TRUST

Fishermen preparing codfish on the Port-au-Port peninsula.

The province of Newfoundland and Labrador was founded largely on the rich bounty in the ocean that laps at its rugged shores. Over the centuries, its economy was built on and prospered largely on the fishery and mostly the abundance of cod.

The Vikings were the first Europeans to use cod as their main source of food during their brief time in Newfoundland around the year 1000. Nearly 500 years later, John Cabot's observation that "the schools of cod in the waters off Newfoundland were so thick that they slowed the ships," set off a veritable "cod rush" in fish-hungry Europe.

The cod catch seemed to know no bounds. In 1962, a total of 1.6 million tonnes of the fish spawned off Newfoundland and Labrador and six years later an all-time record 810,000 tonnes were caught.

In 1977, Canada secured an exclusive 320 km fishing limit off its east coast. Before this time, any Canadian or foreign vessel could fish virtually anywhere off the coast. By 1985, inshore fishers had concerns about declining stocks. In 1992, there were just 22,000 tonnes of the fish spawning off the coast, prompting Ottawa to take the "temporary" step of closing the fishery.

On June 2, 1992, the federal government declared a moratorium on the Northern Cod, effectively putting 19,000 fishers and plant workers, and another 20,000 out of work. The cod fishery has never rebounded and its dismal state stands in sharp contrast to its glory years.

Limited local fisheries were conducted between 1998 and 2002, and again in 2006 and 2007, to assess the cod stocks which some fishermen claimed were on the increase. It appears populations have rebounded in some inshore areas. However, the overall stocks remain at a low level — particularly offshore — and scientists are not optimistic that they will ever recover.

FIVE FAST FACTS

1 After the attack on the World Trade Center on September 11, 2001, air traffic controllers at Gander Airport in rural Newfoundland, used their emergency Y2K plans to help land dozens of transatlantic aircraft making their way to the US. The locals took the stranded passengers into their homes until it was safe to fly again.

2 Newfoundland and Labrador has its own dictionary. The province's language and dialect is so diverse that different communities spread throughout the Island often have their own, unique accent.

3 Newfoundland and Labrador is also the only province to have its own encyclopedia, named Pony and Dog.

4 Newfoundland has a lot of moose…over 100,000, but the large mammals are not native to the Island. Instead, they were introduced over 100 years ago.

5 Saint John's is the eastern terminus of the Trans-Canada Highway.

Newfoundland moose feeding on leaves near Trinity Bay.

CULTURE AND COMMUNICATION

Traditional Toutons on a plate with molasses being poured over.

A NEWFOUNDLAND SCOFF

There is no better way to enjoy an authentic cultural experience than by sampling a region's traditional foods, and there are some delicious and curious culinary items on the menu in Newfoundland.

If you've never had a proper Newfoundland scoff, then you're in for an unforgettable experience. Many of the traditional dishes that were enjoyed by the Island's first settlers still grace the dinner tables today, and they're every bit as interesting as the land from which they come.

Not surprisingly, much of the traditional Newfoundland cuisine includes fish. All manner of fish is consumed here, but the codfish is king, so while other seafood is named accordingly, if you see the word "fish" on the menu, it's codfish they're talking about. Although it's prepared any number of ways — boiled, stewed, au gratin — pan-fried cod is the clear favourite, and you'll find it on the menu just about everywhere you go. Filleted, dipped in milk and flour, and browned in a skillet of pork fat, this ubiquitous dish is a must-try.

Here is a list of some of the more traditional favourites from Newfoundland kitchens,

Halibut with Ginger and Onions — Use fresh halibut and fry in ginger and onions.

Pickled Herring — Makes a great snack or an appetizer.

Fried Cod Tongues — One of the most popular recipes in the province. Use small cod tongues as larger ones have more fat.

Fisherman's Brewis — A traditional dish common all over Newfoundland.

Grand Bank Cod Chowder — Traditional chowder using cod and potatoes.

Bonavista Fish Cakes — Made from using scraps of leftover fish and potatoes.

Blueberry Cobbler — Made from wild blueberries.

Tickle-Hour Raisin Buns — Traditional buns with raisins.

Partridgeberry Cottage Bread or Pudding — Partridgeberries are tart like cranberries and can be found on dry barrens throughout the province.

Bakeapple Pie — Bakeapples are actually tart, yellow berries found on wet barrens. They are considered a delicacy in the province.

Bread Puddin' — Serve hot or cold with cream.

Rhubarb Dessert — A mainstay in most Newfoundland desserts.

Caribou Stew — The traditional stew made with caribou meat.

Roast Partridge — Refers to any of the variety of grouse found in the province.

Moose Stew — Dishes made from moose meat have become popular in the province. For best results, let the meat age between seven and 10 days before cooking.

Broadcove Rabbit Pie — Serve rabbit pie with potatoes, green peas or other vegetables.

Labrador Flipper Dinner — Be careful to clean all the of the seal meat before cooking.

Jigg's Dinner — One of the best-known Newfoundland meals.

Old-Fashioned Baked Beans — Traditionally made and served in logging camps.

Grandma's Toutons — Served with butter and molasses.

Auld-Time Figgy Duff — Serve with heated molasses.

Newfoundland Trifle — Traditional English trifle with a few drops of rum.

Our Mustard Pickles — The best side dish to go with Jigg's Dinner.

Pineapple-Corn Salad — Good way to use leftover corn.

Old-Fashioned Potato Salad — Potatoes mixed with peas and boiled eggs.

Pickled Cabbage — Served as a side dish with any meal.

Rhubarb Relish — Usually eaten with cold canned meats.

Bottled Dandelion Greens — Served as a side dish with boiled meat and potatoes.

Squashberry Jelly — Squashberries grow on trees and make a sweet, red jelly.

Good Ol' Blueberry Wine — Takes two months to age.

Spruce Beer — An old Newfoundland beverage not very common these days.

NEWFOUNDLAND SPECIALTIES

Pease pudding — Also known as Pease pottage or Pease porridge, it is a savoury pudding dish made of boiled legumes, typically split yellow or Carlin peas, with water, salt, and spices, and often cooked with bacon or ham.

Figgy duff — A traditional Canadian bag pudding, made with raisins. One traditional recipe lists the ingredients as breadcrumbs, raisins, brown sugar, molasses, butter, flour and spices. These are mixed and put in a pudding bag, wrapped in cheesecloth or stuffed into an empty can and then boiled, usually along with the cooking vegetables of the Jigg's dinner. For the record, there are no figs in figgy duff.

Fish and brewis — Another highly popular meal, brewis is hard tack, a brick-like, non-perishable biscuit, softened by cooking in pork fat along with the cod. The best part of this meal is the scrunchions, which are small pieces of fat-back pork cooked to a golden crunch. These salty morsels are extremely tasty, and they really make this meal a treat. Fish and brewis can frequently be found on café and restaurant menus.

Cod tongues and cheeks — These are sought-after delicacies. They are removed from the fish, rolled in flour, and fried to a golden brown colour.

Britches — Named for their resemblance to a pair of baggy pants, britches are the roe of the codfish, cooked and served in the original packaging, so to speak. You might say it's the caviar of Newfoundland.

Moose meat — While not native to the Island, moose meat has become a staple of the Newfoundland diet since their introduction around 1904. It is served fried, baked, boiled, stewed and bottled, and enjoyed as steak, honey garlic sausages, and even as burgers.

Blue potatoes — A variety common to Newfoundland and is as pleasing to the palate as it is to the eye.

Lassy mogs and jam-jams — Cookies made with molasses and homemade jam respectively.

Bakeapples, bog-apples or cloudberries — These are the amber-colored berries of a low-growing plant found in Newfoundland bogs. They are popular as jam, or just, as they are, with a generous helping of sugar and cream, and can often be purchased at farmer's markets or souvenir outlets.

Jigg's Dinner — One of the most famous recipes from Newfoundland. Also called boiled dinner or cooked dinner, a Jigg's Dinner is a traditional meal commonly prepared and eaten on Sundays in many regions around the province. Typically, the meal may consist of salt beef, boiled with potatoes, carrots, cabbage, turnip or turnip greens. Traditionally served with Pease pudding and Figgy duff.

Jiggs dinner – a traditional meal of Newfoundland and Labrador.

HISTORY WAS MADE WITH THREE CLICKS

Cabot Tower on Signal Hill in Saint John's.

Built by Samuel Garrison and constructed of local granite between 1898-1900, Cabot Tower was built on Signal Hill in St. John's to commemorate Newfoundland's discovery by John Cabot and Queen Victoria's Diamond Jubilee. Guglielmo Marconi, an Italian inventor and electrical engineer, received the first transatlantic wireless message on December 21, 1901 near Cabot Tower.

Technically, the transmission was received by Marconi in an abandoned fever and diphtheria hospital, located near the tower, which has since been destroyed by fire. The transmission, in Morse code, originated from Marconi's Poldhu Wireless Station located at Cornwall in the United Kingdom.

The distance between the two points was about 2,200 miles (3,500 km). The message was simply three clicks, which in Morse code stands for the letter "S."

Today, Marconi is credited as the inventor of the radio and in 1909, he shared the Nobel Prize in Physics with Karl Ferdinand Braun in recognition for their contributions to the development of wireless telegraphy.

According to the provincial heritage website, Cape Race Lighthouse was the location for Newfoundland's first wireless communication station and was established in 1904, a couple of years after the first transatlantic message was sent by Marconi from Signal Hill.

The lighthouse became a centre for reporting news around the world and the Marconi Wireless Station received a signal from RMS Titanic after the vessel hit an iceberg off Newfoundland waters.

On the night of April 14, 1912, three operators — Walter Gray, Jack Goodwin and Robert Hunston — had taken up their positions at the wireless radio station at Cape Race, a point of flat, fog-shrouded, baron land located at the southeastern tip of the Avalon Peninsula on Newfoundland. The Cape Race station was one of two land-based locations that received the distress call from the RMS Titanic, the other being the Marconi telegraph station on top of the Wanamaker's department store in New York City.

THE PRINTED WORD

The first newspaper published in Newfoundland was the weekly St. John's *Royal Gazette* that started publishing in 1807.

By the 1830s, several weekly and bi-weekly newspapers were established in St. John's and in the major outports. They were highly politicized, reflecting and perhaps aggravating the political, religious and social tensions that periodically upset 19th-Century Newfoundland.

Among Newfoundland's first daily newspapers were the St. John's *Daily News* and Newfoundland *Journal of Commerce* (established 1860), the *Morning Chronicle* (established 1862), the St. John's *Evening Telegram* (1879), the short-lived St John's *Free Press* and *Daily Advertiser* (1877), and *Daily Ledger* (1879).

ON THE AIR

Newfoundland's first public radio stations began operation in St John's in the 1920s. By the 1930s, radio stations were broadcasting throughout the Island. In April 1949, the CBC began its Newfoundland operation and initiated FM broadcasting in 1975.

The province's first TV station, CJON, was opened in 1955. Originally, the station began as a CBC affiliate, but became associated with the national CTV network in 1964 after the CBC opened its own St John's TV studios.

Cable TV on the Island dates from 1977. The largest cable company in the province is Cable Atlantic, which has stations in Corner Brook, Gander, Grand Falls-Windsor, Port aux Basques and St John's.

IT'S FOR YOU

St. John's was the site of Newfoundland's first telephones. They arrived in March 1878, when postmaster John Delany installed two phones he had built using instructions from the magazine *Scientific American*. The phones connected Delany's home with that of a fellow post office employee and were mainly used for post office business.

The province's second phones showed up in 1884 at Archibald's Furniture in St. John's. The first public phone system was established in 1885. Following are other important dates in the evolution of phone service in Newfoundland,
- The annual cost of a residential phone system in 1921 was $30.
- The first long-distance line was installed in 1921.
- The first long-distance call was made on November 27, 1921, between Brigus and Harbour Grace.

- A phone conversation on January 10, 1939 between Governor Sir Humphrey Walwyn and Canadian Governor General Lord Tweedsmuir became the first phone call between Canada and Newfoundland.
- The first dial phone service in Newfoundland appeared in 1948.
- Cellular phone service was first established in Newfoundland and Labrador in 1990.

AT THE MOVIES

The first cinema in Newfoundland was The Nickel. It opened in St. John's in 1907. After that, movie houses soon opened all over the Island and people were lining up to see the latest adventures and romances from Hollywood.

The earliest Newfoundland filmmakers on record were usually hobbyists who used cameras to record local events, family outings, scenery and travels. The first of them may have been Eric Bowring and Judge Harry Winter. The two men from St. John's began collecting footage in 1904.

John Munn, another amateur cameraman, may be the best known of these filmmakers. His work includes footage of a protest at the Colonial Building in 1932 and scenes from Amelia Earhart's visit to Harbour Grace.

One of the few early photographers to see his footage turned into a finished film was a missionary named Monsignor O'Brien. He first came to Labrador in 1928 and continued to visit regularly for the next 20 years, always accompanied by his film camera. In 1979, O'Brien worked with the Memorial University Extension Service to assemble his footage from Davis Inlet and Northwest River into a film called *The Indians' Father Whitehead*.

Films of Newfoundland and Labrador were usually created by producers and directors who arrived with film crews from Canada, Great Britain or the United States. The earliest silent movies associated with the Island are *Moose Hunting In Newfoundland* (1905) by the American Mutoscope and Biographical Company and *Stalking And Shooting Caribou In Newfoundland* (1907) by the Edison Company, though there is evidence to suggest the moose hunting film may have been done elsewhere and subsequently mislabeled. Other companies followed, and for the next 20 years, most of the movies shot in Newfoundland were travelogues designed to promote the Island and Labrador as hunting and fishing destinations.

VARICK FRISSELL

In 1922, an American named Varick Frissell arrived in Labrador as a volunteer with the Grenfell Mission. Frissell worked with the mission for several years, often shooting film of his travels throughout the region. He completed three documentaries about Labrador, including *The Great Arctic Seal Hunt* (1928).

Frissell's fascination with the seal hunt lead him to create the first Hollywood-style sound film ever made in what is now Canada. He wrote a screenplay about two sealers, their rivalry for a woman's love and their adventures on the seal hunt. He formed a company to finance the project and generated interest from several distributors.

With a cast of New York actors and an American film crew, Frissell filmed most of *The Viking* (named for a sealing ship) in Quidi Vidi in 1930. Determined to supplement the story with images showing "the hardihood, skill and courage of the Newfoundland seal hunt," Frissell then took his crew to the Grand Banks and Labrador to collect realistic footage and do the more exciting action sequences.

The Viking debuted with a private showing at the Nickel in March of 1931, but Frissell came away convinced that his movie needed more real scenes from the Labrador ice flows. He assembled another small film crew and within days had joined the real *Viking* for its annual seal-hunting voyage.

On March 15, as the *Viking* sat trapped in ice near the Horse Isles, an explosion in the powder room destroyed the back of the ship and killed 27 men. Frissell's body was never found. That summer *The Viking* was released in Toronto, New York, London and Paris.

For the next 40 years, dramatic films would be rare and unusual occurrences in Newfoundland. In 1941, the British Ministry of Information sent a crew to Canada to make a film called 49th *Parallel* as part of its wartime propaganda campaign. It included a special effects scene in which a German submarine — actually a plywood structure fitted with dynamite and gunpowder — was exploded in waters near Corner Brook.

In 1946, the Newfoundland Commission of Government paid a British company $200,000 to profile the Island and its way of life through a drama called *Island Story*. Cast with local actors and filmed in St. John's, it was released in 1949. St. John's audiences were unimpressed and the film was ultimately seen by few inside or outside the province.

Documentary making increased steadily during the war years and the decades that followed. The National Film Board of Canada first came to the Island in 1940 to make *Toilers Of The Grand Banks*, a nine-minute film about fishermen. The war effort and the Newfoundland lifestyle were the subjects of several other short NFB films in the pre-Confederation years. During the 1950s and 1960s, the board produced over 50 short films and vignettes in the province.

The provincial government began making films in the 1950s and 1960s. Most Newfoundland communities were still without television, so promotional and educational films that could be shown in theatres were seen as important tools for reaching the people. Most of the films provided practical information or celebrated various government programs. They were also used to promote the province to outsiders. The hunting and fishing films of American naturalist Lee Wulff, who had been visiting and filming in the Newfoundland wilderness since the 1930s, were perhaps the most popular government-sponsored films of this era.

TELEVISION AND MOVIES

The first TV drama filmed in Newfoundland was Ted Russell's *The Holdin' Ground* and it began production 1959.

Some of the television series and movies made in Newfoundland and Labrador include:

Codco, (1986), TV Series

Dooley Gardens, (1999), TV Series

Random Passage, (2001), TV Miniseries

This Hour Has 22 Minutes, (1994), TV Series

The Adventure of Faustus Bidgood, (1986), Movie

Anchor Zone, (1994), Movie

The Audience, (2001), Movie

Away from It All, (1961), Movie

Bayo, (1985), Movie

Behind the Red Door, (2002), Movie

The Bingo Robbers, (2000), Movie

The Boys of St. Vincent, (1993) (TV Movie)

The Codfish Industry in Newfoundland, (1911), Movie

Contact, (1997), Movie

The Divine Ryans, (1999), Movie

Encounter at Trinity, (1957), Movie

Eskimos in Labrador, (1911), Movie

Extraordinary Visitor, (1998), Movie

Forty-Ninth Parallel, (1941), Movie, also known as *49th Parallel* and *The Invaders*, (released in the US in 1942)

The Frazers of Cabot Cove, (1949), Movie, also known as *An Island Story*, (1949)

The Grand Seduction, (2013), Movie

The Great Arctic Seal Hunt (1928), Movie, also known as *The Swilin' Racket* (1928)

John and the Missus, (1987), Movie

Labrador, (1919), Movie

Labrador and Newfoundland, (1919), Movie

The Lure of Labrador, (1926), Movie

Misery Harbour, (1999), Movie

My Left Breast, (2000), Movie

Not with My Wife, You Don't! (1966), Movie

Orca, (1977), Movie, also known as *The Killer Whale* (1977) and *Orca, Killer Whale* (1977)

Port aux Basques, (1920), Movie

The Price of Malice, (1916), Movie

Rain, Drizzle, and Fog, (1998), Movie

Rare Birds, (2001), Movie

A Rosewood Daydream, (1970), Movie

The Rowdyman, (1972), Movie

Sea Raiders, (1922), Movie

Seal Hunting in Newfoundland, (1912), Movie

Secret Nation, (1992), Movie

The Shipping News, (2001), Movie

Stalking and Shooting Caribou in Newfoundland, (1907), Movie

Stations, (1983), Movie

The Terry Fox Story, (1983), TV Movie

The Trunk, (1995), Movie

The Viking, (1931), Movie

Violet, (2000), Movie

A Whale for the Killing, (1981), TV Movie

Whales, (1997), Movie

When Ponds Freeze Over, (1998), Movie

LOVE AND MARRIAGE

In the early days of European settlement, marriage was regulated by local custom. Newfoundland and Labrador were sparsely populated and members of the clergy were few in numbers. Unencumbered by English marriage laws, anyone who could read a marriage service could officiate at a Newfoundland wedding.

In the early 1800s, concern grew over this practice and in 1817, Newfoundland's first Marriage Act was written. It stipulated that to be legal, a marriage ceremony had to be performed by an Anglican or Catholic clergyman, or a magistrate.

In 1833, the year after the creation of responsible government, the Newfoundland legislature passed a new Marriage Act allowing clergy of any denomination to conduct marriages.

In Newfoundland and Labrador today, you must be 19 years of age to get married. Today, as well, a marriage license costs $50 and is valid for 30 days. An applicant must wait four days after ordering the license before it is issued. Another four days must pass after it is issued before the officiator can conduct the marriage.

On December 21, 2004, Newfoundland and Labrador began issuing marriage licenses to same-sex couples.

IT'S OFF TO SCHOOL WE GO

The Church of England's Missionary Society for the Propagation of the Gospel in Foreign Parts organized the first schools in Newfoundland. In fact, the first school in Newfoundland was established in Bonavista in the 1720s.

The Society then went on to operate schools in St John's and in several of the larger outports by the 18th Century. According to historical records, these facilities were open to children of all denominations.

A variety of schools were organized in the early 19th Century, the most significant being those operated by the Newfoundland School Society. Established in 1823 with a special concern for educating Newfoundland's poor, by the early 1840s, this society had nondenominational schools in many towns and outports.

The first direct government involvement with education came with the passing of the Education Act in 1836. Through this act, funds were distributed among societies promoting education, and nondenominational boards of education were established.

By 1843, the education grant had more than doubled and was divided between Roman Catholic and Protestant school boards.

According to information found on the Canadian Encyclopedia website, the Protestant grant eventually was distributed among several Protestant denominations. Post-Confederation amalgamation occurred among several Protestant school systems, but government-funded, church-administered education survives today. The denominational education system is protected in the Terms of Union (1948).

Today, with the exception of a few small private institutions, Newfoundland and Labrador's 268 schools are administered by five school boards, one of which, le Conseil Scolaire Francophone, spans the entire province. Boards have the primary responsibility for distributing funding provided by government and religious education programming. Policy decisions are the responsibility of the Department of Education.

In 2015–16, there were 66,800 students enrolled in kindergarten through to grade 12. This represents a 23 per cent decrease in enrollment from 15 years earlier (86,898 students were enrolled in 2001–02).

AFTER SCHOOL ACTIVITY

Founded in 1925 as Memorial University College, Memorial was made the province's only university by a special Act of the House of Assembly (1949). It is located on the outskirts of St John's.

Sir Wilfred Grenfell College, a degree-conferring institute located at the west coast Corner Brook campus of Memorial, was established in 1975. The Fisheries and Marine Institute in St John's became an affiliate of Memorial in 1992. Other post-secondary institutions include the College of the North Atlantic and 26 colleges of applied arts, technology and continuing education.

HALF AN HOUR LATER IN NEWFOUNDLAND

The Newfoundland Time Zone is a geographic region that keeps time by subtracting three and a half hours from Coordinated Universal Time during standard, or subtracting two and a half hours during daylight saving time.

The Newfoundland Time Zone consists only of the province of Newfoundland and Labrador. By legislation, the entire province is officially in the Newfoundland Time Zone. In practice, however, Newfoundland Time is observed only on the Island of Newfoundland, its offshore islands, and southeastern Labrador communities south of Black Tickle.

The remaining areas of Labrador, from Cartwright north and west, observe the Atlantic Time Zone, along with the rest of Atlantic Canada. Southeastern Labrador prefers Newfoundland time, in part to synchronize with the schedule of radio broadcasts from Newfoundland.

This time zone exists because of the location of the Island and the fact that it was a separate dominion when the time zones were established. The Island of Newfoundland lies squarely in the eastern half of the Atlantic Time Zone, exactly three and a half hours from Greenwich. Since it was separate from Canada, it had the right to adopt its own time zone.

While the entire province lies west of the standard meridian for a half-hour time zone, 52.5 degrees west longitude, this is also the near exact meridian of St. John's, the province's capital and largest city. In 1963, the Newfoundland government attempted to bring the province into conformity with the other Atlantic Provinces, but withdrew in the face of stiff public opposition.

This unusual time zone puts the Island of Newfoundland an hour and a half ahead of Central Canada, a half hour ahead of the rest of Atlantic Canada, and half an hour behind Saint-Pierre and Miquelon. Because of this, it will hit milestones of time before (almost) any other part of the continent, a quirk that draws attention to Newfoundland.

In the case of Canada-wide broadcasts timed to air at the same local hour in the rest of the country through the use of a different feed for each time zone (most commonly the CBC's radio and TV networks), Newfoundland uses Atlantic-time broadcasts. References to programs airing at "6:00, 6:30 in Newfoundland" are commonly heard across Canada. However, whenever the province's two stations, CJON and CBNT (both based in St. John's), originate local programming, they usually refer to it as "coming up at 6:00, 5:30 in most of Labrador."

FIVE FAST FACTS

1   Newfoundland was the first province to respond to the *Titanic*'s distress signal.

2   Newfoundland and Labrador is the youngest province in Canadian Confederation.

3   Sheila NaGiera (Magella or MaGeila?) Is she real? Only the undiscovered foggy history of Newfoundland knows for sure. As oral history tells it, she may have been an O'Connor, the daughter of a claimant to the Irish Throne of Connaught. Oral traditions abound in tales of Newfoundland's early Irish Princess. She is reputed to have come to Newfoundland in the early 1600s and married one Gilbert Pike. The couple became planters and small business people in nearby Carbonnear Island in 1611. It is believed they were the first European couple to settle Newfoundland's shores.

4   Newfoundland and Labrador has the lowest rate of divorce in Canada. For argument sake, the Yukon has the highest divorce rate.

5   The first Hindu temple built in Atlantic Canada was in Mount Pearl. In 1975, Hindus established a Hindu temple in Mount Pearl. Swami Chinmayananda donated a marble statue of Krishna which was installed by Swami Dayananda. The temple functioned as an independent organization with the name Chinmaya Mission St. John's. In 1995, a new temple was constructed in the east end of St. John's where most Hindus live, and subsequently it was renamed Hindu Temple St. John's Association. All major Hindu festivals are celebrated in this temple.

DISASTERS

THE CRASH OF ARROW AIR FLIGHT 1285
December 12, 1985
Gander, Newfoundland

Located in the northeastern part of the Island of Newfoundland in the province of Newfoundland and Labrador, Gander is strategically situated on the shores of Gander Lake. The town is the site of Gander International Airport, formerly an important refueling point for transatlantic aircraft.

Gander was chosen for the construction of an airbase in 1935 due to its location close to the northeast tip of the American continent. Construction of the base began in 1936, and the town saw immediate growth and development. During the Second World War, as many as 10,000 people were settled around the airbase. Once the war was over, however, the airbase became a civilian airport and the location of the town was moved a safe distance from the runways. The present municipality was incorporated in 1958.

After the Second World War, the town continued to grow as the airport was used as a refueling stop for transatlantic flights, earning it the name "Cross-roads of the world" as nearly all overseas flights had to stop before crossing the Atlantic.

The Gander airport played an important role in the immediate hours following the September 11, 2001 attacks in the United States when all of North America's airspace was closed by NORAD. In total, 39 trans-Atlantic flights bound for the United States were ordered to land at the airport — more flights than any other Canadian airport other than Halifax International. Vancouver International received the most passengers, at 8,500, but over 6,600 passengers and airline crewmembers unexpectedly found themselves forced to stay in the Gander area for up to three days until airspace was reopened and flights resumed. Residents of Gander and surrounding communities volunteered to house, feed and entertain the travellers in what became known as Operation Yellow Ribbon. This was largely because Transport Canada and NAV CANADA asked that trans-Atlantic flights avoid the major airports in central Canada, like Lester B. Pearson in Toronto and Montréal-Dorval.

Worst air crash in history

However, this was not the first time that Gander had been thrust into the international limelight. December 12, 1985, promised to be a cold and damp day for the island province of Newfoundland. As day broke, a heavy fog hung in the air, embracing everything it touched with a moist hug. In the hours before dawn, freezing rain had pelted the countryside, blanketing most surfaces with a sleek layer of ice. In the minutes just before sunrise, an Arrow Air DC-8 rolled off the runway at Gander International Airport. A few minutes later it crashed into the hillside near Gander Lake, becoming a fiery projectile of death. In an instant, all 256 souls on board were killed, among them 248 American soldiers and eight civilian flight crew.

The article in the December 18, 1985, edition of The Gander Beacon told the story.

The worst plane crash on Canadian soil in history occurred in Gander just before seven o'clock last Thursday morning, December 12, 1985, taking 256 American lives. There were no survivors.

The crash came shortly after the Miami, Florida, Arrow Airlines DC-8 jetliner, under charter to the United States Defence Department, took off from Gander, where it had taken on some 100,000 pounds of fuel. It had left runway 22, which ends near the Trans-Canada Highway, but the plane, carrying 248 members of the 101st Airborne Division to their home base at Fort Campbell, Kentucky, barely made it a quarter-of-a-mile, coming down near Gander Lake. There were also eight crewmembers on board.

The actual location was off a dirt road, known as the boating house road, which is maintained by Transport Canada. The plane struck a small hill, then bellied for some 300 yards, while it split in pieces and the main section came to rest amid intense smoke and fire. Bodies, clothes, luggage and cargo were strewn over the path, left through the wooden area.

The U.S. military personnel, who were returning to spend Christmas with their families at Hopkinsville, Kentucky, had been on assignment as a peacekeeping force in the Sinai Peninsula of Egypt. The plane had left Cairo, Egypt, then stopped over at Cologne, West Germany, before continuing on to Gander. At the time of the crash, weather was overcast and there had been freezing rain overnight.

A search began into the cause of the crash, as a 300-member search team arrived from Washington and Ottawa. The black box flight recorders were found but were damaged, so there was no immediate indication of what caused the crash.

For Gander, it was quite a week, as the tragic and traumatic drama unfolded. News reporting teams from all parts of North America descended on Gander, the likes of which were never seen before. The scene was closed as search officials feared for explosions, concerned there was ammunition aboard the aircraft. There was nothing removed from the crash site until the following Friday. A hangar served as a makeshift morgue.

Investigation into the crash was the responsibility of the Canadian Aviation Safety Board and there would be a public inquiry. In Beirut, an anonymous caller, who claimed to be representing the Islamic Jihad organization, said this group caused the crash. There was another such claim, as well, but all were dismissed by both the RCMP and United States government officials.

The soldiers who died in the crash were members of the Third Battalion, 202nd Infantry at Fort Campbell. It was the worst air crash in Gander since 1967, when a Czechoslovakian plane went down, killing 38 people.

The official story has it that Arrow Air Flight 1285, a MacDonnell Douglas DC-8 crashed after taking off from Gander International Airport at 6:45 a.m. in Newfoundland on December 12, 1985. It took nearly four hours for the firefighters who responded to bring the blaze under control because of the large amount of fuel on board — the plane was flying direct from Gander to Fort Campbell in Kentucky. It was more than a day before the flames were completely extinguished, according to a historical summary released by the Department of the Army in 1986.

All passengers on board were American Servicemen returning from the Mount Sinai region. Most were members of the 101st Airborne Division (Air Assault). They had just completed a six-month tour of duty in the Middle East with the Multinational Force and Observers, a peacekeeping force made up of parties from 10 different countries. The force had been responsible for enforcing the security provisions contained in the 1979 Israeli-Egyptian peace accord.

Investigation results

The Canadian Aviation Safety Board immediately began an investigation into the crash. Initially, it was believed that a combination of factors, not the least of which was ice on the wings might have contributed to the crash. However, further investigation by a nine-member panel failed to come to a truly definitive conclusion as to the cause of the crash.

The majority, five members, believed that there was sufficient evidence to indicate that, shortly after takeoff, the aircraft stalled because of excess drag, possibly the result of ice, creating an untenable situation in which the aircraft was, for all intents, doomed — especially given the amount of fuel on board. However, four other members (which included two aeronautical engineers according to a Time Magazine article from 1992), believed that there was sufficient evidence uncovered by the safety board to indicate that the Arrow had suffered some sort of on-board catastrophic event that resulted in a loss of power. The loss of power could have been the result of a fire or the detonation of an on-board explosive device. Part of the evidence indicated there had been a pre-crash fire on board and autopsy reports that revealed some soldiers had inhaled smoke before perishing.

The nine-member Safety Board was nearly split on the matter of the probable cause of the accident. The five-member majority supported the official report, which concluded that the cause of the sequence leading up to the stall and crash could not be determined, with icing a possibility. The four-member minority opinion, however, was that the crash was possibly caused by detonations of unknown origin in a cargo compartment which led to an in-flight fire and loss of control of the aircraft,

"... We cannot agree — indeed, we categorically disagree — with the majority findings ... The evidence shows that the Arrow Air DC-8 suffered an on-board fire and a massive loss of power before it crashed ... The fire may have been associated with an in-flight detonation from an explosive or incendiary device."

The Town of Gander marked the twentieth anniversary of the air crash tragedy with a special ceremony on December 12, 2005. The event included a wreath laying at the Silent Witness Memorial which has been built at the crash site near Gander Lake.

The death toll from the Arrow disaster constituted the deadliest plane crash in Canada (as of 2006) and was the highest death toll on any day for the U.S. armed forces since the Second World War, even including combat losses, the greatest of which occurred in 1983, after the Marine barracks bombing in Beirut.

Those servicemen who died were from the following divisions, all but twelve were members of the 3d Battalion, 502d Infantry, and 101st Airborne Division (Air Assault); eleven were from other Forces Command units; and one was a CID agent from the Criminal Investigations Command.

THE BELL ISLAND BOOM
April 2, 1978
Avalon Peninsula, Newfoundland

The Bell Island Boom occurred on April 2, 1978. It is reputed to have been a large explosion or disruption and left in its wake many damaged homes in the vicinity of Bell Island, located off the Avalon Peninsula of Newfoundland.

The explosion, of unknown origin, while causing no fatalities, did produce significant property damage and created two saucer-shaped holes in the rocky ground at the impact site. According to reports, these holes measured at between two and three feet in width. The blast was heard 45 kilometres away and American Vela satellites picked up the event.

Bell Island is only about 34 square kilometres in size and sits in Conception Bay. It is, essentially, a 20-minute drive, followed by a 20-minute ferry ride from St. John's. The Isle's famed iron ore mine, known as the No. 2 Mine, closed in 1949, but for years boosted the local economy, with a total of 79 million tons of ore having been extracted during 71 years of mining operations on the Island. It was, for a time, the British Commonwealth's largest producer of iron ore. Today the mine has been converted into a tourist attraction.

Interestingly, Bell Island was among the few places in North America to see, first-hand, the ramifications of wartime combat during the Second World War when, in 1942, German U-boats torpedoed a pier loaded with iron ore, taking out four other vessels in the process. Upwards of 8,000 tons of ore had been stored at the pier and was awaiting shipping to other locales. A total of 69 people died during the attack. Today, there is a Seamen's Memorial located at Lance Cove at the southern end of the Island to commemorate those who lost their lives during the Second World War-era U-boat assaults.

While Bell Island had its days of excitement during the war, an event some 36 years after Nazis roamed the coastline proved disturbing in nature for what it may represent technologically. According to Tom Bearden, a retired colonel and nuclear engineer who conducted extensive research on the history of electromagnetic weapons, the Bell Island Boom of April 1978 was initially blamed on a ball of lightning.

The focal point for the incident occurred over the Bickfordville area of the Island, located on the southwest side of the Island. According to what Beardon found, an unusual beam of what locals believed was lightning came directly down (not jagged like lightning usually is) from the sky at a 45-degree angle to the ground. The lightning vaporized wires leading to a nearby shed and that structure, along with a nearby coop, suffered damage, but there was no evidence of burning consistent with most types of known lightning strikes. The bolt also reportedly did not discharge into metal contact points. A number of television sets in the nearby settlement at Lance Cove reportedly exploded at the time of the supposed lightning strike.

The event attracted American scientists from a weapons research facility in Los Alamos and led to speculation that Americans may have been testing some sort of electromagnetic-based weapon over Newfoundland during this Cold War-era event, Beardon notes. This was according to the news media reports at the time.

Beardon is among those who vehemently subscribed to the belief that the ball of lightning was, in fact, a Cold War-era electromagnetic weapons test. Beardon also notes meteorological reports at the time that indicate atmospheric conditions on that April day in 1978 were not conducive to the development of lightning over the Avalon Peninsula. Another notation suggested that the impact of the blast was heard 45 kilometres away in Cape Broyle.

According to the Tour Bell Island website, the holes left behind by the ball of lightning are still evident in the ground today, nearly 30 years later.

ST. JOHN'S KNIGHTS OF COLUMBUS HALL FIRE
December 12, 1942
St. John's, Newfoundland

The story hit the front page of the St. John's *Evening Telegram* on December 14, 1942, two days after the event. It told of death and destruction unlike anything the people of this small Newfoundland city had seen before, or since.

About 500 people were having a good time on a blustery cold Saturday night at the Knights of Columbus Leave Centre on St. John's Harvey Road when, just after 11 p.m., the music came to an abrupt stop.

Shouts of "Fire! Fire!" suddenly rang through the building and panic gripped the air. The fear was palpable. People tried to escape the inferno, but to no avail, as many of the exits and all windows were covered over as part of wartime blackout regulations. Within five minutes, anybody still left in the flimsy building was dead, burned alive or quickly overcome by smoke and gases from the inferno. A total of 99 deaths occurred with over 100 injuries. The fire station was less than a kilometre away, but that didn't matter, as the hall went up like a tinderbox. There was little chance of rescue.

Even though, when the blaze happened, Newfoundland was not yet a part of Canada, since joining the country in 1949, the Knights of Columbus Hall blaze ranks among the deadliest structure fires in Canadian history.

According to Robert Parsons, who specializes in the history of Newfoundland's small fishing communities along the province's south coast, among the victims was Private Bertram Baker, a member of the Newfoundland Regiment. He was among the dearth of servicemen in the hall attending the dance that night when the fire struck. He perished in the blaze and, today, his name can be found inscribed on a bronze plaque at Grand Bank Memorial Library. Baker was one of at least four individuals from the community of Grand Bank to perish in the fire. Fellow serviceman Pte. George Lambert and civilians Emma Hickman and Rose Thorne also died in that night's mayhem.

Parsons, who wrote about the stories of Newfoundland in his book, Born Down by the Water, says the St. John's fire was a disaster of unequaled proportions even by today's standards. "It left a legacy of death and destruction, along with a mystery that has not been solved to this very day. There was widespread speculation about the cause of the fire including that it was arson or some other form sabotage, but nothing was ever proven. Even an inquiry that followed the fire failed to produce any clear evidence that the blaze had been deliberately set. To this day people will say the fire was set by a spy working against the Allies during the war, but that theory has never been backed up by any proof."

This Knights of Columbus Hall Fire was the swiftest and deadliest indoor fire in the annals of Canadian disasters. It was even more spectacular than Montreal's Laurier Palace Movie Theatre fire of January 9, 1927, when 76 children suffocated to death while trying to escape up the narrow theatre aisles in panic.

The St. John's fire was devastating and many in the community believed the blaze was almost certainly lit by an enemy agent, who, according to local legend, cunningly used rolls of toilet paper as his torch, but as Parsons points out, these types of stories often stem from such a tragedy. "It is true that the city may have been a target for spies working in the war effort, he concedes. "But was a spy responsible for this deadly fire? I don't know. ... It seems the cause will remain a mystery forever."

St. John's, because of its strategic location as the first major port in North America at this time in history, was a veritable hotbed of intrigue. The port city was a rallying point for European-bound Allied convoys and so it was swollen with servicemen and infested with enemy agents of all stripes.

Rumours of subterfuge and sabotage by a German agent were rampant in the community for some time after the December 12 fire, but such innuendo was never conclusively proven. Today, the cause for one of Canada's deadliest structure fires in history remains a mystery, buried in the dust of time.

SINKING OF THE *OCEAN RANGER*
February 15, 1982
The Atlantic Ocean off the Coast of Newfoundland

An article that appeared in the newspaper, *Sunday Express*, following the sinking, called it, "The great silent moan that arose from one end of the province to the other." It seemed that the tragedy had practically touched the entire province of Newfoundland. Of the 84 men on board the Ocean Ranger when it went down, 69 were Canadian and of them, 56 were Newfoundlanders.

At the time, the *Ocean Ranger* tragedy was the world's second-worst catastrophe in offshore drilling history (next to the 1980 North Sea tragedy, when 123 died). The *Ocean Ranger*'s demise may not have slowed the petroleum industry in Newfoundland, but it did remind those involved of the dangers that come with it. It offered a wake-up call to the industry.

The *Ocean Ranger* was designed by Odeco Engineers of New Orleans. Promoted as the biggest rig in the world and weighing more than 14 thousand tonnes, the Ocean Ranger was built by Mitsubishi Heavy Industries in Japan. It first operated in the Bering Sea off Alaska in 1976. From there it moved to New Jersey, then Ireland and in November 1980, arrived on the Grand Banks amid much fanfare as politicians heralded its arrival as the beginning of a new era for Newfoundland — the era of oil. The *Ocean Ranger* was a massive oil rig touted as unsinkable and able to drill in areas too dangerous for other rigs. She was the pride of the offshore oil industry, the biggest rig of her day.

Although there are reports of the crew referring to the rig as "the Ocean Danger," it was considered the safest on the water. "It had a kind of Titanic reputation," said one weather observer who had spent eight months on the rig, while speaking to a reporter for the weekly newspaper, The Express. "We were told it was the 'Unsinkable *Ocean Ranger*.' It was designed for use anywhere in the world, in every weather condition."

The *Ranger* was one of three semi-submersible rigs — all under contract to Mobil Oil Canada — drilling at the time on the Hibernia oil field, about 200 kilometres east of St. John's. The structure was basically a drilling platform held in place by huge anchors that rested on two pontoons that floated just below the surface of the water. Each was longer than a football field. To stabilize the immense rig, 24 ballast tanks and six pumps were contained in the pontoons. By pumping seawater in and out of the tanks, the ballast operator could keep the rig level while loading equipment from a supply ship, or during rough weather.

On Sunday, February 14, a vicious storm developed south of Newfoundland and headed for the Grand Banks. By sunset that day, winds were up to 90 knots and seas were building rapidly. At around seven o'clock, with seas over 30 metres high, the main deck of the *Ocean Ranger* reported an especially huge wave. Sometime after seven o'clock, the *Ocean Ranger* reported to the mobile shore base in St. John's that a giant wave had crashed over the rig smashing a porthole in the ballast control room. Water rushed in and shorted out circuits. As a result, the rig began to list.

No one on board could stop what was happening. At five minutes past one on Sunday morning, February 15, they requested that the supply ship come close and stand by. Four minutes later, the Ocean Ranger sent an SOS signal to search and rescue.

"We're listing badly and we need to get the seamen off the rig," it said. Another call from the Ocean Ranger states, "We may not be able to hold the rig, rig might fall over..."

Tragedy

At half past one, the *Ocean Ranger* signaled it was sending its crew to lifeboats. That was the last time anyone heard from them. By two o'clock, supply boats in the area had come to rescue people, or at least try. Despite their best efforts, however, all rescue attempts failed and all crew members perished. At almost 20 minutes to four that morning, Coast Guard and other rescuers watched their radars in utter horror and disbelief as the *Ocean Ranger* disappeared.

All 84 crewmembers on board died. Over the next four days search teams were only able to recover 22 bodies, two lifeboats, and six life rafts. Autopsies showed those men had drowned. A royal commission looked into the disaster. It concluded the *Ocean Ranger* had design flaws, particularly in the ballast control room, and that the crew lacked proper safety training and equipment.

Launched within months of the *Ocean Ranger*'s demise, the royal commission was jointly established and funded by the governments of Newfoundland and Canada. The $16-million, three-year project was assigned the dual task of examining what happened the night the rig capsized and formulating recommendations to ensure it would never happen again.

The first volume of the commission's final report points at design flaws, inadequate training and poor safety provisions as causes of the accident. Volume two outlines 136 suggestions to improve the safety and accountability of the industry. It describes the need for tougher Canadian safety and inspection standards for rigs, improved workersafety, emergency response planning and training, design changes and increased competency among industry workers.

Some very important lessons were learned from the sinking of the *Ocean Ranger*. Some of those lessons were focused around the technology and the safety of the platform. The tragedy of the *Ocean Ranger* made the oil companies and other participants respond in many different ways. The government has continually examined the safety issues that contributed to this disaster of the *Ocean Ranger* and has implemented numerous changes to enhance the safety of the offshore workforce. The royal commission on the *Ocean Ranger* disaster concluded that the deaths resulted not only from the storm and flaws in the rig's design, but also from a lack of human knowledge.

According to an *Ocean Ranger* website, experts say the many deaths could have been prevented with better safety training and better safety precautions. Since then, new and old rules have been enforced. One rule that was not enforced in the past was that a worker had to be carrying a special card, which indicated that they have passed all tests for the job in the past three years. Without this card, they would not be allowed to board the helicopters that take workers to and from the rigs.

As well, during the late 1980s, the Federal and Provincial governments installed boards to regulate offshore oil and gas. These boards required anyone visiting the rigs to have minimum safety training. Over the past two decades, survival systems have improved greatly in offshore drilling. Some of the new technologies that were introduced include cold-water survival suits and improved methods of lifeboat deployment. Also for more safety, training requirements for offshore workers have increased intensely and new facilities have been established to make sure that the workers have the safety skills to avoid another big accident like the sinking of the *Ocean Ranger*. As well, weather buoys were established in selected locations throughout the waters in Atlantic Canada to provide critical weather information to forecasters and mariners.

The oil companies were held liable because their workers weren't trained for emergency procedures and didn't do any emergency drills. It was felt that the *Ocean Ranger* could have survived the storm and flooding if those in charge had understood how the ballast system worked. The *Ocean Ranger* did not have enough safety equipment on board for the amount of passengers it had. Families of lost crewmembers sued the companies that owned and operated the *Ocean Ranger*. In turn, they were forced to pay out millions in lawsuits.

On the twentieth anniversary of the sinking of the *Ocean Ranger*, the Government of Newfoundland and Labrador released a message ensuring to those affected that major changes have been made to the oil and gas industry,

"Major legislative and regulatory changes were made to the Atlantic Accord Acts by the Federal and Provincial governments to establish strict safety guidelines that must be followed from the initial design of an offshore project to the actual implementation of safety systems during the operations phase of development. These regulations govern the necessary requirements of offshore safety.

"Over the past two decades, government and industry players have worked together to ensure that the necessary funding is available to facilitate the important research needed to improve escape, evacuation and rescue systems. New technologies have been introduced including cold-water survival suits and improved methods of lifeboat deployment. Training requirements for offshore workers have increased significantly and new facilities have been established to ensure that these workers have the necessary safety skills to avoid tragedy."

SINKING OF *TITANIC*
April 14, 1912
The North Atlantic Ocean

"We are unable to conceive of any disaster occurring to this vessel because modern shipbuilding has gone beyond that sort of thing."

— *Edward J. Smith, Captain of* RMS Titanic

On the night of April 14, 1912, three operators — Walter Gray, Jack Goodwin and Robert Hunston — had taken up their positions at the wireless radio station at Cape Race, a point of flat, fog-shrouded, baron land located at the southeastern tip of the Avalon Peninsula on Newfoundland. The Cape Race station, built in 1904, was the first wireless station in Newfoundland. It would be one of two land-based locations that received the distress call from the *RMS Titanic*, the other being the Marconi telegraph station on top of the Wanamaker's department store in New York City.

There had been reports throughout the day of icebergs being spotted in the north Atlantic shipping lanes. Ships, including the *Baltic*, another White Star liner, had been sending out warnings advising of large ice flows in the region. It was at Cape Race that the first hint of any problems with *Titanic* was heard.

The wireless station at Cape Race was 400 miles west of *Titanic*'s location when the first indications of impending disaster were heard by the three men stationed there. After the first distress call, Robert Hunston started a message log. *Titanic*'s shipboard time was one hour and 50 minutes ahead of Eastern Standard Time which was used at Cape Race. *Titanic* first used the distress call CQD, which stands for Come Quick Distress, later adding the new code, SOS.

April 14th

- 10:25 p.m. (EST) [12:15 a.m. on *Titanic*]

    J.C.R. Goodwin on watch hears *Titanic* calling C.Q.D. giving position 41.44 N 50.24 W about 380 miles SSE of Cape Race.

- 10:35 pm

    Titanic gives corrected position as 41.46N 50.14W. A matter of five or six miles difference. He says "have struck iceberg".

- 10:40 pm

    Titanic calls *Carpathia* and says "We require immediate assistance". Gray on duty.

- 10:43 pm

  Titanic gives same information to *Californian*, giving *Titanic*'s position.

- 10:45 pm

  Caronia circulates same information broadcast to *Baltic* and all ships who can hear him. RH on duty.

- 10:55 pm

  Titanic tells German steamer "Have struck iceberg and sinking".

- 11:00 pm

  Titanic continues calling for assistance and giving position.

- 11:25 pm

  Establish communication with *Virginian* here and give him all information re, *Titanic*, telling him to inform captain immediately. OK.

- 11:36 pm

  Olympic asks *Titanic* which way latter steering. *Titanic* replies "We are putting women off in boats".

- 11:55 pm

  Virginian says he is now going to assist *Titanic*. *Titanic* meanwhile continues circulating position calling for help. He says weather is calm and clear.

April 15th

- 12:50 am

  Virginian says last he heard of *Titanic* was at 12:27 a.m. when latters signals were blurred and ended abruptly. From now on boats working amongst themselves relative to *Titanic* disaster. Nothing more heard from *Titanic*.

- 2:05 am

  First message from New York asking for details. This is followed by about 300 more, chiefly from newspapers to many ships asking for news.

After Daylight

- News commences to arrive from ships stating *Carpathia* picked up 20 boats of people. No word of any more being saved.

THE NEWFOUNDLAND TSUNAMI
November 18, 1929
The Burin Peninsula, Newfoundland

Tsunami — a Japanese word meaning "harbour wave"

"Suddenly without warning, there is a roar of waters. Louder than that of the ordinary waves on the shore, it breaks on their ears, and then, with a shuddering crash, a fifteen-foot wall of water beats on their frail dwelling, pouring in through door and window and carrying back in its undertow, home and mother and children!"

— The November 22, 1929 editorial in the St. John's Daily News

The Burin Peninsula region of Newfoundland was first given the name Buria by Basque fishermen centuries ago. Buria, for those unfamiliar with the term, is an old Russian word that carries the meaning "tempest," so it should come as no surprise that the small swath of land off the south coast of Newfoundland, known for its poor weather and rough conditions, acquired the name. But what washed ashore on November 18, 1929, was no storm. No, it was a force of nature much more powerful. At that time, keep in mind, Newfoundland was not yet part of Canada, but was instead a self-governing dominion.

The University of Washington Department of Earth and Science has an on-line collection of reports detailing and studying the impacts and causations of tsunamis. A tsunami is generally something associated with the Pacific Ocean, so any occurring in the Atlantic Ocean would be considered unique, indeed. The product of undersea volcanic eruptions, landslides, earthquakes or a combination thereof, tsunamis are massive, fast-moving waves that propel outward from an epicentre, wreaking havoc on whatever land they may encounter in their path.

On November 18, 1929, just after 5:00 p.m. local time, a major earthquake occurred off Newfoundland's coast on the Grand Banks, a major fishing ground that fueled the province's economy. The resulting disturbance, which also included a major underwater landslide, registered a score of 7.2 on the Richter scale, strong enough to be felt as far away as Montreal and New York City. Transatlantic telegraph cables were affected as was regular shipping traffic. The result of the tsunami was observed across the breadth of the Atlantic as far away as Portugal. The quake's epicentre was at 44'69 north and 56-degrees west, about 250 kilometres away from the nearest land — Newfoundland's Burin Peninsula.

The three tsunami waves produced from the underwater eruption came ashore along the Burin Peninsula around 7:30 p.m. local time and left a swath of destruction unlike anything seen before. According to the Library and Archives of Canada, the waves were travelling at a speed in excess of 129 kilometres an hour. More than 40 tiny hamlets and coastal fishing communities were swamped by the disturbed brine.

It took three days for emergency supplies to begin arriving in the region and relief was prevented from reaching the affected areas by a blizzard that struck the day after the waves. The loss of property because of the tsunami eventually came in at a total of over one million dollars, a substantial figure in those days. Over 10,000 people were left homeless. One of the 28 reported deaths connected with the tsunami occurred on Cape Breton Island, where the force of the wave was also felt in certain coastal areas.

Losses

While the immediate impact of the tsunami was eventually tabulated in terms of monetary loss and human suffering, the long term effects of the tidalwave were felt for decades. For instance, in the wake of the tidal wave, the local fishing industry was all but decimated as the earthquake and resulting tsunami destroyed the once fertile fishing grounds of the Grand Banks.

There was very little fish left on the Burin Peninsula for about 10 years after the tidalwave because for six or seven years after there were no squid and as squid was the bait fish for cod, it meant if there were no squid, then there were no cod. And if people couldn't fish, they couldn't survive. It's something that often goes over looked when people are discussing the tsunami, but this was the beginning of the Great Depression and people had it hard. The collapse of the fishery left these communities with little hopes of recovery from such a disaster.

On January 23, 2007, the Federal government announced the activation of the Atlantic Tsunami Warning System. At a press conference in Halifax, Nova Scotia, the Honourable Stockwell Day, the then Minister of Public Safety, said, "The security of Canadians is a priority of Canada's new government. The devastating tsunami in southeast Asia heightened concerns about tsunami warnings in coastal areas around the world. Today, I'm pleased to announce that we are taking action to strengthen our security by activating a warning system for tsunamis along Canada's East Coast."

The new Atlantic tsunami warning system uses the same equipment and procedures already in place to issue storm surge warnings to government agencies, the media and the public. In fact, the enhancements made to the existing system to allow tsunami warnings, will also improve the capacity to predict storm surges, which are much more frequent events on the East Coast.

Day explained that this system brings together Canada's state-of-the-art earthquake monitoring networks with the best alert technologies available in Atlantic Canada. Earthquakes, whether centered under land or sea, could have a dramatic impact on coastal communities, and systems such as this allow authorities to quickly alert eastern Canadians to potential hazards.

The tsunami warning system is led by the Department of Fisheries and Oceans (DFO), and is the result of collaboration between the Federal Departments of Natural Resources, Environment Canada, and Public Safety and Emergency Preparedness, with provincial emergency management agencies in the five easternmost provinces and the U.S. National Oceanographic and Atmospheric Administration (NOAA). It anticipates the development of an international system for issuing tsunami warnings for the Atlantic and Indian Oceans, similar to the one existing for the Pacific Ocean.

The new system will continue to be refined and enhanced as technology improves.

Why develop a system?

On December 26, 2004, a magnitude 9.0 earthquake occurred off the coast of Indonesia. This triggered destructive tsunami waves that impacted the coasts of Indonesia, Thailand and Sri Lanka, as well as other countries in the Indian Ocean region. There was both an international and Canadian response to this tragedy.

Here in Canada, it was recognized the East Coast lacked a tsunami warning system. While the West Coast receives tsunami warnings via the internationally-coordinated Pacific Tsunami Warning System, there was no equivalent system for the Atlantic Coast. Even though over 70 per cent of tsunami events occur in the Pacific Ocean, due diligence demands that some detection and warning capability also be available on Canada's Atlantic Coast and Gulf of St. Lawrence. It is important to remember the most devastating Canadian tsunami originated on the Grand Banks in 1929 — leaving 29 people dead, many people homeless, and 50 communities affected in Newfoundland and Labrador and Cape Breton Island, Nova Scotia.

THE 1914 SEALING DISASTER
The North Coast

While the Newfoundland and Labrador spring sealing industry was a lucrative venture, it was also more hazardous than any other local fishery at the turn of the 20th Century. To find their catch, sealing ships had to steam each year into the dangerous ice floes off Newfoundland's north coast, where large frozen masses of floating seawater and sudden blizzards could jam ships in the ice and crush their hulls. Five steamers were lost between 1906 and 1914, reducing the country's sealing fleet to 20 vessels. In no other fishery did ships enter the floes.

Once on the ice, the men faced additional dangers. Carrying little food, no shelter, and dressed in clothing ill-suited for sudden squalls, the sealers might spend up to 12 consecutive hours on the ice. Because their ships could only maneuver a limited distance into the ice fields, the men often had to walk for miles before reaching any seals. If the unpredictable North Atlantic weather worsened, the men would have to turn back and fight their way through blinding snow and fierce winds, guided to safety by the sound of their ship's whistle.

Although quick to help, captains of other vessels often did not know when crews, other than their own, were in trouble because of the great distances separating ships. While the sealing fleet had encompassed upwards of 400 sailing ships in the early 1800s, the introduction of giant steamers with their large crews in the late 19th Century had thinned the fleet considerably and forced vessels to be more widely spaced throughout the ice floes. Some ships carried wireless apparatus to aid in communication, but the costly equipment was not mandatory and often considered unnecessary by ship-owners.

Inevitably, the dangers inherent to the Newfoundland and Labrador seal fishery — augmented by human error or negligence — resulted in numerous deaths and accidents. The most horrific of these occurred in 1914, when 251 of the country's sealers died in two separate but simultaneous disasters involving the *SS Newfoundland* and *SS Southern Cross*.

These tragedies were immediately seared into the public consciousness and ultimately prompted government officials to change the way they regulated the seal fishery.

SS Newfoundland

Although the *Newfoundland* disaster resulted in fewer deaths than that of the *Southern Cross*, its shocking details sparked a more intense and emotional response from the public. For two days, 132 sealers were stranded on the ice in blizzard conditions and without adequate shelter. Almost two-thirds of the men died and many of the survivors lost one or more limbs to frostbite.

However, when the *SS Newfoundland* left St. John's for the North Atlantic ice fields in March 1914, no one anticipated the hardships that lay ahead. Its captain, Westbury Kean, was accompanied on the hunt that year by his father Abram Kean, veteran sealer and captain of the *SS Stephano*. Although the two ships worked for competing firms, each captain had agreed to alert the other of any seals they spotted by raising their after derrick — a type of wooden crane found on marine vessels.

On March 30, the powerful steel steamer *Stephano* had navigated its way deep into the ice fields where it found a herd of seals. Abram Kean ordered his derrick raised, but the *Newfoundland* — a weaker and less maneuverable wooden steamer — was jammed in the ice between five and seven miles to the south and could not proceed. Frustrated by his inability to move and anxious to catch a share of the seal herd, Westbury Kean ordered his men off the ship the following morning. He instructed them to walk to the *Stephano*, believing the sealers would spend the night onboard his father's steamer after a day of hunting. Although the sky was cloudy, Kean did not anticipate bad weather as the morning was mild and the ship's barometer gave no indication of a brewing storm. The *Newfoundland*, however, was not carrying a thermometer and Kean could not tell if the temperature was falling or rising.

Nonetheless, 166 men jumped onto the ice and headed for the distant *Stephano* at 7 a.m. As the morning progressed, many of the sealers recognized signs of an approaching storm and talked uneasily about the weather. At about 10:00, 34 men decided to turn back, the remaining 132 reached the *Stephano* by 11:30. Abram Kean invited the men on board and offered them a lunch of tea and hard bread. He mistakenly believed that the group had left the *Newfoundland* at 9 a.m. and had only been walking for two hours. While the men ate, Kean navigated the *Stephano* towards a group of seals two miles to the south. Although it was snowing quite hard, Kean ordered the men off his ship at 11:50, with instructions to kill 1,500 seals before returning to the *Newfoundland*. He did not invite them onto the *Stephano* for the night.

Tired from the morning's four-hour trek, unable to see the *Newfoundland*, and in a thickening storm, the 132 men were once again on the ice. The group's leader, George Tuff, did not object to Kean's orders and the *Stephano* steamed away to pick up its own crew members hunting in the north. By 12:45 the blowing snow forced the sealers to stop hunting and head for their own ship. Walking through knee-deep snowdrifts and across wheeling ice pans, the men continued until dark, when Tuff ordered them to build shelters from loose chunks of ice. This, however, proved ineffectual against the night's shifting winds, sudden ice storms, and plummeting temperatures. Many men died before morning, others could barely walk, their limbs frozen and numb.

The group spent the next day and night trying to reach the *Newfoundland*, but without luck. Some men, delirious, walked into the frigid waters and drowned, others were pulled back onto the ice by their companions, but often died within minutes. Westbury and Abram Kean, meanwhile, each believed the sealers were safely aboard the other man's ship. Communication between the two vessels was impossible because the *Newfoundland* was not carrying wireless equipment. The steamer's owner, A.J. Harvey and Company, had removed the ship's wireless because it had failed to result in larger catches during previous seasons. The firm was interested in the radio only as a means of improving the hunt's profitability and did not view it as a safety device.

It was not until the morning of April 2 that Westbury Kean, surveying the floes through his binoculars, spotted his men crawling and staggering across the ice. Desperate to help, but lacking any flares, Kean improvised a distress signal to alert other vessels within the fleet. Soon, crewmen from the *SS Bellaventure* were on the ice with blankets, food, and drink. The *Stephano* and *SS Florizel* also helped in the search. Of the 77 men who died on the ice, rescuers found only 69 bodies. The remaining eight had likely fallen into the water.

SS Southern Cross

While the 132 men of the *Newfoundland* were stranded on the ice in the North Atlantic, a second sealing tragedy was unfolding to the south. In late March or early April 1914, the *SS Southern Cross* sank while returning to Newfoundland from the Gulf of St. Lawrence, taking with it 173 men.

On March 31, the coastal steamer *SS Portia* passed the *Southern Cross* near Cape Pine, off the southern Avalon Peninsula. Although the *Portia* was headed for St. Mary's Bay to wait out a worsening blizzard, the *Southern Cross*, low in the water with its large cargo of seal pelts, seemed headed for Cape Race. The steamer was not seen again, and because no wireless equipment was on board, communication with other vessels was impossible.

However, it is believed that the ship's heavy cargo may have shifted suddenly in the stormy waves and capsized the steamer. Whatever the cause, the sinking of the *Southern Cross* resulted in more deaths than any other single disaster in Newfoundland and Labrador sealing history.

In 1915, the government held a commission of inquiry to examine the *Newfoundland* and *Southern Cross* sealing disasters. Although it laid no criminal charges, the inquiry found Abram Kean, Westbury Kean, and George Tuff all guilty of errors in judgment. In Tuff's case, the inquiry felt he should have refused the orders of Abram Kean, one of the most powerful men in the seal hunt, to return with his watch to the *Newfoundland*.

More importantly, the commission recommended that all sealing vessels carry wireless sets, barometers, and thermometers, and that ship owners be held accountable for any injuries or deaths sustained by their crews. In 1916, the government passed legislation prohibiting sealers from being on the ice after dark and requiring all sealing ships to carry wireless equipment and flares. In response to theories that the *Southern Cross* sank because of overloading, the government also made it illegal for any ship to return from the hunt with more than 35,000 pelts.

St. John's harbor and downtown seen from Signal Hill.

FIVE FAST FACTS

1 St. John's is the only city in the country with radio stations whose call letters do not begin with the letter "C," which is the International Telecommunication Union (ITU) prefix for Canada. ITU prefixes for the Dominion of Newfoundland were "VO" and three AM stations in the province kept their existing call letters after 1949.

2 The fishing village of Renews on the Avalon Peninsula once served as a pit stop for the Pilgrims' ship, Mayflower. During the ship's 66-day voyage to Plymouth Rock in 1620, it docked at Renews to pick up water and supplies to complete the journey.

3 Water Street in St. John's was first used in the early 1500s, making it the oldest commercial Street in North America.

4 People from more than 100 countries and speaking more than 70 different languages live in Newfoundland and Labrador.

5 The highest peaks of Newfoundland and Labrador are all found in the Torngat Mountain range that borders the province of Quebec. The highest peak reaches 1,652 meters while the lowest rises to 1,204 meters, about one-eighth the height of Mount Everest.

FAMOUS NEWFOUNDLANDERS AND LABRADOREANS

Lights. Cameras. Action!

While Newfoundland and Labrador is a long way from Hollywood, the place where dreams of stardom are fulfilled, many of the province's sons and daughters have followed their dreams there. Some have gone on to find fame in the movies and on television.

Natasha Henstridge was born on August 15, 1974 in Springdale, Newfoundland. She is best known for her staring roles in movies such as the 1995 science-fiction thriller, *Species* and the comedy *The Whole Nine Yards* in 2000. Henstridge started her career as a model in Paris, France at the age of 15. After leaving home to begin her modeling career in the highly competitive Paris fashion world, she landed her first cover of French *Cosmopolitan* and graced the covers of many international fashion magazines, appearing in commercials for Oil of Olay, Lady Stetson and Old Spice.

Pursuing her love of acting, at age 19, Henstridge landed the starring role in *Species* opposite Academy Award winning actors Sir Ben Kingsley and Forest Whitaker. The film became a worldwide hit critically and commercially and Henstridge received praise for her performance as the genetically modified Sil, including an MTV Award.

This began a recognized film career that has spanned over 35 movies to date. Henstridge has proven herself to be a versatile and fearless actress. She won the Best Actress Gemini Award (Canada's equivalent of an Emmy Award) for her hard-hitting portrayal of a policeman's wife in the 2008 miniseries *Would Be Kings* and starred with Geena Davis in the 2005 Golden Globe-winning series *Commander in Chief*. Her television credits include leading roles in *She Spies* (2002) and *Eli Stone* (2008). In 1997, she also voiced Miss Ellen on the animated series *South Park*. She returned to movies in 2016 in the period drama, *The Bronx Bull*, playing the wife of legendary boxer Jake LaMotta.

Henstridge is the youngest actress to receive the Lifetime Achievement Award from the Temecula Film Festival. She is married to actor and platinum-selling recording artist Darius Campbell. They live in Los Angeles, California with her two children, and are involved in humanitarian efforts including St Jude Children's Research Hospital, World Vision and Fresh2o water charity.

Actor Joanne Kelly was born in 1978 in Bay d'Espoir. She grew up on the south central coast of Newfoundland and Labrador but left to attend Acadia University in Nova Scotia at the age of 17. Her performances include roles in a variety of films including *The Bay of Love and Sorrows* (2002), *Crime Spree* (2003), *Mafia Doctor* (2003), *Going the Distance* (2004) and the 2002 TV series *Jeremiah*. She now lives in Vancouver.

Sara Canning was born on July 14, 1987 in Gander. She is known for her work on the TV series *The Vampire Diaries* (2009), *The Right Kind of Wrong* (2013) and *Eadweard* (2015).

Shannon Tweed was born in St. John's and rose to stardom as Miss November 1981 for Playboy magazine. She also appeared in the soap opera *Falcon Crest* in 1981 and began her movie career the following year. She became Playmate of the Year in 1982 and was briefly involved with Playboy magazine founder Hugh M. Hefner. She has carried on a long-term relationship with Gene Simmons, front man for the rock band KISS, since 1983. The couple married in 2011 and have two children. The family starred in the reality television show, *Gene Simmons, Family Jewels* from 2006 to 2012. Tweed has become somewhat of a "B" movie queen, appearing in numerous low-budget erotic thrillers and adventure films.

Movie director and producer, Brad Peyton was born in 1979 in Gander. He is known for the Hollywood films *San Andreas* (2015), *Journey 2, The Mysterious Island* (2012) and *Cats & Dogs, The Revenge of Kitty Galore* (2010).

Actress Jennifer Hale was born on January 1, 1972 in Goose Bay. She is best known for her performances in *Mass Effect 3* (2012), *Star Wars, Knights of the Old Republic* (2003) and *Cinderella II, Dreams Come True* (2002).

Born in 1968 and raised in Wabush, Shawn Doyle has become a familiar face to audiences worldwide, turning out critically acclaimed performances on both the big and small screen.

With his move to Los Angeles in 2005, Doyle quickly amassed an impressive list of credits with recurring roles on the series *Desperate Housewives* (2004) and *24* (2001). He also had guest starring roles on *Lie to Me* (2009), *Terriers* (2010), *Dark Blue* (2009), *Lost* (2004), *Numb3rs* (2005) and *Blind Justice* (2005). In 2010, he said goodbye to his regular role as Joey in the hit series *Big Love* (2006) to portray the brilliant, charismatic and egocentric Balagan in *Endgame* (2011).

Prior to moving south, Doyle starred in the critically-acclaimed Canadian series *Bury the Lead* (2002) and received the 2002 ACTRA Award and a 2004 Gemini (Canadian Emmy) nomination, both for Outstanding Male Performance In A Leading Role, and a 2005 Gemini nomination for Outstanding Performance In A Guest-starring Role. He starred opposite Mary-Louise Parker in the 2007 CBC/BBC movie *The Robber Bride*, which garnered him a Gemini Award for Outstanding Male Performance In A Dramatic Program Or Miniseries. His other Canadian television credits include the CBC miniseries *Guns* (2008), *The City* (1999) for which he received a Gemini nomination, *Scar Tissue* (2002), *A Killing Spring* (2002) for which he received a Gemini nomination), *Criminal Instincts* (2000), *Peacekeepers* (1997) and the miniseries *Dieppe* (1993). He will soon be starring as the Father of Canadian Confederation, John A. Macdonald in the movie, *The Rivals*.

Doyle's film credits include *Grown Up Movie Star* (2009), *White Out* (2008), *Sabah* (2005), *Don't Say a Word* (2001), *Frequency* (2000), *The Majestic* (2001), *Knockaround Guys* (2001) and *Mount Pleasant* (2006). On stage, Doyle has performed in a long list of plays, both contemporary and classical. His most recent outing in Carol Churchill's *A Number*, earned him the 2006 Dora (Canadian Tony) Award for Outstanding Male Performance.

Born December 9, 1969, in St. John's, Sebastian Spence is most notably recognized as "Cowboy" Cliff Harting in the Hallmark Channel's television series Cedar Cove, which started production in 2013. Currently living in Vancouver, Spence has become one of the most sought-after actors in BC. As the son of playwrights Janis Spence and Michael Cook, Spence was destined to have a career in the world of acting from the beginning. He was bitten by the acting bug at an early age, and his first role in *The Boys of St. Vincent, 15 Years Later* was met with critical acclaim.

Following this role, he was thrust into television roles and made-for-television films. That was until his first true starring role on the science fiction original series *First Wave* from 1998-2001. Throughout his career, he guest-starred in a variety of science fiction television shows, made-for-television films, and on occasion these turned into recurring guest spots (*Dawson's Creek* and *G-Spot* most notably). He also received prominence for the role of Timmy Callahan in the four Donald Strachey mystery films opposite Chad Allen.

A native of Bell Island, and a graduate of the National Theatre School of Canada, Allan Hawco, who was born in 1977, is one of the country's most exciting and recognizable stars. As co-creator, Hawco wrote, executive produced and stared in the hit CBC television drama/comedy *Republic of Doyle*. Hawco played Jake Doyle, the roguish and irreverent private investigator at the center of a colourful cast of characters who live and work together as an extended family while they try and run a P.I. racket in St. John's.

Republic of Doyle ran on CBC in Canada for six seasons and has been sold to markets all around the world including a syndication deal across America. *Republic of Doyle* was produced by his company, Take the Shot Productions, which is currently in production of their new Netflix original series, *Frontier*, in which Hawco plays fur trader, Douglas Brown.

In 2005, Hawco co-founded and is still currently the co-artistic director of The Company Theatre in Toronto. He produced and starred in its inaugural production of Tom Murphy's *Whistle in the Dark*, which met with rave reviews. Hawco was singled out for his performance as well.

The Company Theatre has gone on to produce numerous productions such as *Domesticated*, *Bellville*, *Festen* and the Dora Award winning *Through the Leaves*. Hawco is the recipient of the Canadian Film and Television Hall of Fame Outstanding Achievement Award and the National Theatre School's Gascon-Thomas Award. He is based in St. John's where he lives with his wife, journalist Carolyn Stokes.

Gordon Pinsent was born on July 12, 1930, in Grand Falls. He was known as "Porky" as a child, and dreamed of performing as early as he can remember. He served with the Royal Canadian Regiment from 1948-51. Pinsent received an L.L.D. from the University of Prince Edward Island in 1975, an honorary doctorate from Queen's University in 1988, as well as an honorary doctorate from Memorial University of Newfoundland and the University of Prince Edward Island.

Pinsent left Newfoundland at the age of 17 and began his career on stage. His first theatrical experiences were in Winnipeg, Manitoba. While there, he was involved in the first live radio drama out of Winnipeg. He eventually moved east, working in

Toronto and Stratford, Ontario. He has since won numerous credits and awards, and is one of Canada's most well respected artists.

In addition to acting, Pinsent also directs and produces, and has written a number of novels and screenplays, as well as plays for the stage, including *Corner Green* for the Newfoundland amateur drama festival. The play was staged in St. John's in April of 1997, and was based upon life in his hometown of Grand Falls, Newfoundland. He is a member of the Honorary Advisory Board for the Newfoundland Symphony Youth Orchestra, and is very active in various charities. He wrote about his life in his humorous and poignant autobiography, *By the Way*.

Pinsent is married to actress Charmion King, who he met during his early theater days. She died on January 6, 2007, in Toronto. He has a daughter, actress Leah Pinsent, from that union, as well as a son and daughter from an earlier marriage.

Alan Doyle was born on May 17, 1969 in Petty Harbour. As a singer/songwriter, Doyle rose to fame as the lead singer of Newfoundland and Labrador's traditional Irish-folk/pop band Great Big Sea. He is known for his work on films including *Robin Hood* with Russell Crowe (2010), *State of Play* (2009) and *The Shipping News* (2001). In 2005, he produced the album titled *My Hand, My Heart* for Academy Award winning actor Russell Crowe and co-wrote several songs for that album with Crowe, including a tune titled Raewyn.

Born and raised in Newfoundland, Karyn Dwyer attended theatre school in Toronto. She is perhaps best known for her starring role as Maggie in the hit independent film, *Better Than Chocolate*. In addition, she wrote and starred in her feminist one-woman show *Bad Girls* at the Rivoli, as well as playing Phoebe in *As You Like It* for the internationally acclaimed theatre festival at the DuMaurier World Stage.

Dwyer is the creator/producer/writer/director/star of the tongue-in-cheek web series *First World Problems* (in collaboration with Albert Howell, writer for *The Tonight Show starring Jimmy Fallon*). Other film and stage roles include Lorne Michael's *Superstar*, MIFF Independent Spirit award winner, *Last Call Before Sunset*, the title role in Native Earth's *Romeo and Juliet*, performance artist Sooze in Eric Bogosian's *SubUrbia*, and the role of Carrie, a junkie prostitute in the innovative and experimental, *Exercises in Depravity and Suffragette Koans*.

She was also the lead Rosebud in the TV series *Rosebud's Guide to Seduction*, as well as starring in roles in *Republic of Doyle* and *This is Wonderland*. She also starred in the award winning short films *Pony*, *Polished* and *Dying Like Ophelia*, all directed by

Ed Gass-Donnelly. Her most recent work includes the lead in *The Silent Garden, A Trip to the Island* and *Burning, Burning*.

Born on January 1, 1972, in Burlington, Gemini award-winning actor and comedian Shaun Majumder was raised in rural Newfoundland. He started performing as a teenager and has been at it ever since. His work has taken him through the world of theatre, stand-up comedy, improv, and to his role as Andrew Palmer on the television series *The Firm*, starring Josh Lucas and Juliette Lewis. In 2010, Majumder starred as Detective Vik Mahajan in the critically acclaimed crime drama *Detroit 1-8-7* on ABC.

HBO's *Every Word is Absolutely True*, which follows Majumder as he embarks on his first national stand-up tour, garnered critical praise for its candid look beyond the public persona to reveal his more intimate and complex side in this feature length documentary. In January 2013, his documentary series called *Majumder Manor* debuted on the W Network in Canada. The show was about his dream to transform his rural hometown of Burlington into a high end, sustainable tourist destination.

Majumder's television career has included starring in the Farrelly Brothers comedy *Unhitched*, as well as roles on *24*, Cedric the Entertainer Presents on Fox, *Robson Arms* on CTV, and *Da Kink in My Hair* on Global. In addition to his multiple appearances on *22 Minutes*, he has appeared in *Hatching, Matching and Dispatching* and *Republic of Doyle* for CBC Television. His Comedy Central Presents special also debuted on Comedy Central in 2008.

His film credits include *Harold and Kumar Go to White Castle*, *The Ladies Man*, *Pushing Tin*, *Purpose*, and *Bob Funk* alongside Rachel Leigh Cook and Olympia Dukakis. Majumder is also a favourite of Montreal's Just for Laughs Comedy Festival, having hosted the TV series for three seasons. He resides in Los Angeles.

Writer and actor Mark Critch was born in St. John's. He is well known for his work on The Halifax Comedy Fest (2002), CBC's *This Hour Has 22 Minutes*, *This Hour Has 22 Minutes, New Year's Eve Special* (2003) and *Decline of the American Empire* (2012).

Rick Mercer was born on October 17, 1969 in St. John's, as Rick Vincent Mercer and is one of Canada's most recognized entertainers. He is a writer and actor, known for *The Industry* (1998), *The Rick Mercer Report* (2004) and *Talking to Americans* (2001).

The satirical on-the-street interviews with real Americans demonstrated America's general ignorance of Canada. This gimmick reached its height in 2000 when Mercer interviewed then-presidential candidate George W. Bush and got Bush to congratulate newly elected Canadian Prime Minister "Jean Poutine." (The PM's name was actually Jean Chretien, while poutine is a Canadian dish.)

Comedian Mary Walsh was born on May 13, 1952 in St. John's as Mary Cynthia Walsh. She is a writer and actress, known for *The Rosie O'Donnell Show* (1996) and *This Hour Has 22 Minutes* since 1992. She was one of the original founders of the legendary Newfoundland sketch comedy show, *Codco*, in 1986.

Florence Paterson was born on November 3, 1927 in St. John's. As an actress, she was known for films such as *Little Women* (1994), *It* (1990) and *Bird on a Wire* (1990). She died on July 23, 1995 in Vancouver.

Andy Jones was born on January 15, 1948 in St. John's. He is an actor and writer, known *For The Adventure of Faustus Biggood* (1986), *Rare Birds* (2001) and *Codco* (1986).

Cathy Jones was born on April 6, 1955 in St. John's, as Catherine Frederica Theresa Jones. She is a writer and actress, known for *This Hour Has 22 Minutes* (1992), *Codco* (1986) and *The Grand Seduction* (2013).

Ruby Holbrook was born on August 28, 1930 in St. John's, as Ruby Elaine Johnston. She is an actress, known for *All My Children* (1970), *The Goodbye Girl* (1977) and *Love, Ludlow* (2005). She was previously married to actor Hal Holbrook.

The only daughter of Matthew and Alice (Fitzpatrick) Delaney, Helen Frances Theresa Delaney was born on June 5, 1912, in St. John's. Her father, Matthew, of English-Irish ancestry, was an adventurous merchant seaman.

Unlike many parents who tell their children this, she really did walk several miles to school daily, including through the snow. Helen was born with an eye affliction that doctors said would result in blindness, but when her beloved father died, her mother took to New York in 1925 for a series of eye operations.

The fact that her vision became normal may have helped to lead Helen to realize that hard-luck cases should never be given up as lost. But a different sort of unhappiness struck after she married Fred Martini and they tried to have a child. When the baby was lost, doctors told her she would never have another. Instead, she turned her mothering instincts to animals.

Martini was a jeweler, but they visited the Bronx Zoo regularly. They both loved animals, and with Helen's encouragement he quit his job to become a zookeeper. When he was put in charge of the Lion House, their lives changed forever, and for the better. When a lioness refused to mother its cub, Helen brought it to their New York apartment and raised it herself. She named him after war hero General Douglas MacArthur.

Because of her successful care, the cub was returned to the zoo at the age of two months, and next the officials asked her to rear a litter of tiger cubs. Again Helen saved their lives, and the story was followed closely in the news media, until at the age of three months, they went back to the zoo.

There was no going back now. Unstoppable, she converted a storeroom at the Lion House into a nursery, where she could care for cubs whose mothers were too intimidated by captivity to nurse them properly. Helen was officially hired in August 1944 as the first and only woman zookeeper in the Bronx Zoo. Helen continued to treat cubs at home when necessary, as in the case of the black leopard Bagheera (named after the famous leopard in the *Jungle Books* by Rudyard Kipling).

Helen Martini grew famous in New York for treating animals in her apartment — sometimes despite the complaints of neighbours — including gorillas, marmosets, baby deer, antelope, squirrels and skunks. She did all of this without any special training, simply relying upon books that she read and her own instincts and love.

The public got to share when one of the tiger cubs she had raised had problems with a baby in her own (seventh) litter. Helen allowed zoo-goers to watch as she fed the sickly little cub she called Fer (Hindustani for tiger), along with the first jaguar cubs the Bronx Zoo had ever exhibited. This was in 1954.

Helen got vindication for her mothering when, again in front of the public, she approached the Lion House and the 600-pound Bengal tigers flung themselves on the floor, rolled, purred and begged to be petted. The newspapers also reported that Bagheera "streaked to the bars" and clutched her around the neck, as "the crowd gasped and fell back," then patted her cheeks with "desperate affection."

Helen never claimed to be particularly brave. She was simply taking care of her little ones. She died in Gladstone, New Jersey, in January 1994.

Bill Clark was born on May 20, 1944 in St John's, as Jr. Walter W. Clark. He is a writer and producer, known for *America, A Tribute to Heroes* (2001), *Brooklyn South* (1997) and *NYPD Blue* (1993). Prior to working on NYPD Blue, Clark was a long time homicide detective for the New York City Police Department. The stories on the show were in large part derived from his experiences on the cases he worked on and his observations of the behaviour of suspects.

Tommy Sexton was born on July 3, 1957 in St. John's. He was an actor and writer, known for *The Wonderful Grand Band* (1980), *Codco* (1986) and *The National Doubt* (1992). He died on December 13, 1993 in St. John's.

Greg Thomey was born on May 8, 1961 in St. John's. An actor and writer, he is known for *This Hour Has 22 Minutes* (1992), *This Hour Has 22 Minutes, New Year's Eve Special* (1998) and *This Hour Has 22 Minutes, New Year's Eve Special* (2003).

Gwynne Dyer was born on April 17, 1943 in St. John's. He is a writer and actor, known for *War* (1982), *The Profession of Arms* (1983) and *Paradise Lost* (1994).

Greg Malone was born on October 19, 1948 in St. Johns. He is an actor and writer, known for *Codco* (1986), *The Adventure of Faustus Bidgood* (1986) and *Rare Birds* (2001).

Seamus O'Regan was born on January 18, 1971 in St. John's. He is an actor and producer, known for *Canada A.M.* (2001-2011), *One x One Gala* (2007) and *White House Down* (2013).

O'Regan worked as an assistant to former Environment Minister Jean Charest in Ottawa and to former Justice Minister Edward Roberts in St. John's. He was policy advisor and speechwriter to the Premier of Newfoundland and Labrador, Brian Tobin.

He received his Master of Philosophy degree from the University of Cambridge, England.

In 2007, O'Regan became the first journalist to be named to Canada's Top 40 Under 40 list.

In September 2014, O'Regan was nominated as the Liberal Party candidate in the Newfoundland Labrador riding of St. John's South-Mount Pearl. He defeated the NDP incumbent in the October 19, 2015, federal election that saw the Liberal Party form a majority government under leader Justin Trudeau.

John Murray Anderson was born on September 20, 1886 in St. John's. He became famous as a director, producer, songwriter and author.

Educated at Edinburgh Academy in Scotland and Lausanne University in Switzerland, he studied drama with Herbert Beerbohm Tree. During the Second World War, he served in the American Bureau of Information.

On Broadway, Anderson directed and wrote the scores for *Greenwich Village Follies* (five editions) and *Jack and Jill*. He directed *What's In a Name?* (also librettist and producer), *The League of Notions* (London), *Music Box Revue of 1924*, *Dearest Enemy*, *John Murray Anderson's Almanac* (1929, also producer, 1953), *Bow Bells* (London), *Fanfare* (London), *Ziegfeld Follies* (1934, 1936, 1943), *Life Begins at 8:40*, *Thumbs Up!*, *Jumbo*, *One for the Money*, *Two for the Show*, *Laffing Room Only*, *Three to Make Ready*, *New Faces of 1952*, and *Two's Company*.

He was the director at Radio City Music Hall in 1933, at the Great Lakes Exposition in Cleveland in 1937, at Billy Rose's Diamond Horseshoe from 1938-1950, and for Ringling Brothers Circus from 1942-1951.

Anderson joined ASCAP in 1950 and his chief musical collaborators included Mitchell Parish, Walter and Jean Kerr, and Joan Ford. His popular-music compositions include *The Girl in the Moon*; *Eileen Avourneen*, *That Reminiscent Melody*, *The Valley of Dreams*, *The Last Waltz*, *Come to Vienna*, *Some Day When Dreams Come True*, *A Young Man's Fancy*, *At the Krazy Kat's Ball* and *Annabell Lee*.

In the 1920s, along with partner Robert Milton, he ran an acting school in New York City. Among their students were Bette Davis and Lucille Ball.

Anderson died of a heart attack on January 30, 1954, in New York.

Michael Coady is an award-winning actor, producer, writer, working between LA, Toronto and his native Newfoundland. As an actor, he has made guest star and co-star appearances on shows such as the BBC America series, *Copper*, *The Lottery* on Lifetime Network, CBC series *Murdoch Mysteries* and *Republic of Doyle*, CMT series *Angels Among Us*, History Channel series *Zero Hour*, National Geographic Channel *Valentine's Day Massacre*, and *1000 Ways to Die* on Spike TV.

Coady's credits include the short films *By Water's Edge* (screened at the 2011 Cannes Festival), *The Historian Paradox* (won Audience Choice Award at the Big Island Film Fest in Hawaii), *Silent Night in Munice* (with R.D. Call), (*Into the Wild*, *Babel*, *State of Grace*, screened at the Action on Film Festival in Los Angeles), and the multiple award winning web series *Dead Grandma*.

His theater credits include the Toronto productions *Evita*, *Cabaret*, and the Canadian premiere of *Urinetown*. He also produced and starred in the East Coast Canadian premiere of *Doubt* in 2008.

Coady is the executive director for Canada of We Make Movies, a film collective in Los Angeles and Toronto. He continues to write and produce his own projects like *Obsession* (which he also starred in) and his upcoming short screenplay *Cop Out*, a winner of the We Make Movies Canada (WMM-CA) Screenplay Competition, was chosen as one of WMM-CA's Slate One Films.

Acclaimed writer, journalist and broadcaster, Linden MacIntyre was born on May 29, 1943 in St. Lawrence, Newfoundland, and is best known for *If Justice Fails* (2007), *The Fifth Estate* (1981) and *Frontline* (1983).

MacIntyre has won eight Gemini Awards, an International Emmy and numerous other awards for writing and journalistic excellence, including the 2009 Scotiabank Giller Prize for his 2009 novel, *The Bishop's Man*. Well known for many years for his stories on CBC's *The Fifth Estate*, in 2014 he announced his retirement from the show at age 71. His final story, broadcast on November 21, 2014, was *The Interrogation Room* about police ethics and improper interrogation room tactics.

Kimberly French was born in 1967 in Gander. She has worked on a long list of Hollywood blockbusters as the still photographer including *Power Rangers* (coming in 2017), *Star Trek Beyond* (2016), *The Revenant* (2015), *Tommorrowland* (2015), *Seventh Son* (2014), *Godzilla* (2013), *Red Riding Hood* (2010), *Cats & Dogs, The Revenge of Kitty Galore* (2010), *The Twilight Saga, Eclipse* (2009), *The Twilight Saga, New Moon* (2009), *The Imaginarium of Doctor Parnassus* (2009),

The Uninvited (2009), *The Assassination of Jesse James by the Coward of Robert Ford* (2007), *Shooter* (2007), *Everest*, TV mini-series (2007), *Brokeback Mountain* (2005), *The Lazarus Child* (2005) and *Halloween, Resurrection* (2002). French has done a great deal of work on various TV movies and series including *Karroll's Christmas* (2004), *Family Sins* (2004), *It Must Be Love* (2004), *The Death and Life of Nancy Eaton* (2003), *Undercover Christmas* (2003), *Hollywood Wives, The New Generation* (2003), *We'll Meet Again* (2002), *Skate* (2001), *Just Deal* (2000) and *Ice Angel* (2000).

Actor and writer, Michael Ricketts was born in St. John's on March 3, 1992. He began his acting career when he moved to Ontario to live with his father. After applying to work at a local Starbucks, he was discovered by his current agent as talent and as a spokesperson for one of her novel characters soon to be made into a feature known as *Don't Tell Me Goodbye* (2014). The character was named Alex Hunt.

He was cast in Carrigan Publishing & Productions first short film, *Blind Faith - The Short* (2014) and the web-series *CPP Unveiled* as host. He also worked on a project called *Morning After and a Bottle of Whiskey* (2014).

Walter Learning was born on November 16, 1938 in the small village of Quidi Vidi when Newfoundland was still an independent nation. At the age of eleven, along with 321,000 of his fellow Newfoundlanders, he became a citizen of Canada. At about the same time, he was saved from drowning by an American serviceman, who was fishing off the village pier. It is very likely that the young soldier never realized his great contribution to the future of Canadian theatre.

Before beginning his career path, Learning honed his work experience as a plumber's apprentice and a used car salesman. These skills, especially the latter, would prove valuable when he settled on a career in the performing arts. In 1957, Learning went to the University of New Brunswick (UNB) in Fredericton. Upon receiving his BA, he was awarded a teaching fellowship to pursue his MA, and a Commonwealth Scholarship to work on his PhD at the Australian National University in Canberra.

Learning returned to Canada in May of 1966. He was director of drama at the UNB Summer Session and in the fall returned to Memorial University of Newfoundland. He became a lecturer in the Philosophy Department, where he remained for two years.

In May of 1968, Learning moved back to Fredericton to become the general manager of the Beaverbrook Playhouse. There he founded Theatre New Brunswick (TNB), which presented its first production in January of 1969. TNB was, and is, Canada's only full time touring regional theatre.

He remained as general manager of The Playhouse and artistic director of Theatre New Brunswick for ten years. During that time, TNB produced more than 85 productions. In June of 1978 he left Fredericton for Ottawa to take the position of head of the Theatre Section of the Canada Council for the Arts.

Learning remained at the Canada Council until 1982 when he moved to the West Coast to become artistic director of the Vancouver Playhouse. After five years, he returned back east to Prince Edward Island where he became the artistic director of the Charlottetown Festival. During his career, he has also guest directed at many theatres including the Stratford Festival, the Dallas Theater Center, Persephone Theatre, Festival Antigonish, Lighthouse Theatre, Bastion Theatre and others.

He has also been a frequent director at Australia's Canberra Repertory Theatre. He has appeared as an actor at many theatres across Canada and has guest-starred in a number of television shows and films. From 1992 to 1995, Learning was a freelance broadcaster, writer, actor and director. In 1995, he returned to Theatre New Brunswick as executive producer. He left this position in 1999, and as of 2016, he was still freelancing as an actor and director.

Learning received the Playhouse Honours award in 2011. This annual award recognizes individuals who have made a significant contribution to community life through their work in the performing arts.

Born in Avondale (Middle Arm) on August 1965, Glen Gregory Doyle has been involved in filmmaking since 1987, studying at Ryerson University for Screenwriting and Theatre Arts and subsequently Humber College for Print, Radio, and Television Journalism.

Many of his written works have been produced and published worldwide. He wrote the feature film *Sometimes a Hero* (released in the US under the title Cold Vengence), and *The Circuit*. Both projects were internationally distributed. The success of *The Circuit* lead to demands from international buyers for *Circuit 2* and *Circuit 3, Street Monk*.

Aside from his original works, Doyle was contracted by Silverthorne Pictures in Toronto to adapt the novel *Brotherhood of the Red Rat*, which is now currently in pre-production. He is also the author of the non-fiction book *The Martial Artist's Way* (1999), published by Harper Collins in Canada and Tuttle Publishing in the U.S.

In addition to his writing achievements, Doyle is also an accomplished martial artist with worldwide recognition (a former three-time Canadian Kung Fu Champion). He can be seen hosting and demonstrating in the instructional DVD *60 Minutes to Learn Kung Fu*. He has also worked as an action and fight choreographer for Cynthia Rothrock, and credited for all fight choreography in the film *Sometimes a Hero*.

Doyle has been featured on the cover of numerous international magazines including *Inside Kung Fu*, *Black Belt Magazine*, *World of Martial Arts*, and has made personal appearances on radio shows and numerous television talk shows. He also served as a feature writer for *Canadian Martial Arts Magazine*, and has given lectures to aspiring screenwriters studying at Ryerson University in Toronto.

In May of 2005, he was named Head Coach for the Kung Fu Division of the WKA Team Canada (World Karate Association), after three of his students finished first, second, and fourth at the Canadian National Championships and qualified for the national team.

CBC commentator and author Rex Murphy was born in March 1947 in St. John's, where he graduated from Memorial University.

According to the CBC website, in 1968, Murphy, a Rhodes Scholar, went to Oxford University (along with former U.S. president Bill Clinton). Back in Newfoundland, he was soon established as a quick-witted and accomplished writer, broadcaster and teacher.

Murphy's primary interest is in language and English literature, but he also has a strong link with politics. He is noted throughout Newfoundland for his biting comments on the political scene and his television tussles with prominent politicians, including premier Joey Smallwood, became required viewing for a huge audience.

Murphy gained an insider's view of the political scene when he worked as executive assistant to the leader of the Liberal Party of Newfoundland. To get an even closer taste of politics, Murphy ran twice for office in provincial elections and lost both times.

He has worked extensively with CBC and from Newfoundland he has contributed many items on current affairs issues. For The National he has done a number of documentaries, including the highly acclaimed *Unpeopled Shores*, as well as interviews with immensely popular authors, the late Frank McCourt of *Angela's Ashes*, among them.

Once a week Murphy offers commentary on *The National*'s Point of View, and is additionally the host of CBC Radio's long-running *Cross Country Checkup*. He also writes Japes of Wrath, his Saturday column for *The Globe and Mail*.

Murphy is a commentator on *Definitely Not the Opera*, and has contributed to *Morningside*, *Land and Sea*, *The Journal*, *Midday* and *Sunday Report*. He has won several national and provincial broadcasting awards.

Singer Kim Stockwood was born on November 11, 1965 in St. John's. As an actress, she is known for her performances in *Rise Up, Canadian Pop Music in the 1980s* (2009), *This Beat Goes On, Canadian Pop Music in the 1970s*, and *The Magical Gathering* (2004).

Nick Wall was born on December 18, 1906 in Conception Bay. He was an actor, known mostly for his role in the 1940 film, *That Gang of Mine*. In addition to his short acting career, Wall is mostly remembered as a Canadian jockey who raced at home and in the United States where he competed on the East Coast and in California.

One of his most notable races took place in 1938 when he rode the horse Stagehand to victory over the legendary Seabiscuit in the Santa Anita Handicap. Also that year, Wall was the leading money-winning jockey in the U.S.

He was inducted into Canada's Sports Hall of Fame in 1979. He died on March 17, 1983 in Bellerose, New York.

Born in Brigus, Newfoundland on August 15, 1875, Captain Bob Bartlett followed his family's profession of fishing and seal hunting. In 1905, he was appointed to command Robert E. Perry's ship *Roosevelt* for the explorer's expedition to find the North Pole.

He again commanded the *Roosevelt* in Perry's successful 1908 expedition. During this expedition, Bartlett went as far north as 87 degrees North while bringing supplies to the final expedition party made up of Perry, Matthew Henson and a group of First Nations people who accompanied them. For this, Perry and Bartlett won the National Geographic Society's Gold Medal (Henson, who was Black, received the Hubbard Medal posthumously in 2000).

In 1913, Bartlett commanded the Karluk for Steffanson's Arctic Expedition. The Karluk was crushed in the ice and Bartlett led the survivors to safety on Wrangel Island. He then set out with a single Inuit companion to reach civilization and arrange their rescue. The official history of the Canadian Coast Guard states that,

"Bob Bartlett turned disaster into triumph in the finest feat of leadership in Canadian marine history."

During the First World War, Bartlett commanded transports for the U.S. Navy. Between 1925 and 1946, he participated in twenty arctic expeditions in his schooner the Effie M. Morissey.

Bartlett played the sealing ship captain in the movie, *The Viking*. However, he was not part of the group that went to film additional footage and was lost when their ship blew up. Bartlett, who loved poetry and classical music, never married. He died in New York of pneumonia on April 28, 1946.

Singer Damhnait Doyle was born on December 9, 1975 in Labrador City. The phonetic spelling of her first name (which is Irish) also serves as the title of her 2003 album. She was a member of the band Shaye from 2003 to 2009 with Kim Stockwood and Tara MacLean (who left the group in 2007). She is now part of new group that goes by the name, The Heartbroken.

Ron Hynes, a popular folk singer-songwriter, was born in St. John's on December 7, 1950. A critically acclaimed and award-winning entertainer, he was especially known for his composition, *Sonny's Dream*, which has been recorded worldwide by countless artists. The song was named the 41st greatest Canadian song of all time on the 2005 CBC One series, *50 Tracks: The Canadian Version*. Hynes died November 19, 2015.

FIVE FAST FACTS

1 Newfoundland and Labrador is home to 22 species of whales, the largest being the humpback whale.

2 There were no chipmunks on the Island before 1962.

3 No place on the Island of Newfoundland is further than 100 km from the sea.

4 The people of Upper Cove Island, near Conception Bay, commemorate February 3 as Coombs's Day. On that date over 200 years ago, several members of the local Coombs family perished in a snowstorm.

5 Speaking of snow, Gander received over 50 cm of snow during the Victoria Day weekend in 2015, while the previous year, temperatures had been a pleasant 17 degrees.

FASCINATING FACTS

ONE FOR THE RECORD BOOKS

James Foster McCoubrey may not exactly be a household name in Newfoundland but when he died on July 5, 2013, he was the oldest living man in the world at the time.

An article which appeared on July 10, 2013 in the East Bay Times following his death, said that James Foster McCoubrey, at age 111 acknowledged as the oldest living man in California — and possibly in the world — died Friday in Walnut Creek from natural causes.

McCoubrey had been a contender for recognition as the oldest man in the world since June 12, 2013, when the man who previously held that designation died in Japan.

"I think he was very proud of the fact he lived that long," said Patricia Salveson, McCoubrey's only child and a Walnut Creek resident. "He said, 'I must have good genes!'"

Born in St. John's, Newfoundland, on September 13, 1901, he grew up in that area and later in Massachusetts. His formal schooling ended in the eighth grade, when he went to work to help support his family, later taking high school classes at night. He enlisted to fight in the First World War, but he was underage, and his mother foiled his plan on the eve of his departure to Europe, said granddaughter Beth Salveson of Walnut Creek.

He spent his working life in the insurance business and for many years operated a heating oil business in Massachusetts. He moved to Walnut Creek in 1992 after the death of his wife, Rose, to live with his daughter and son-in-law. He and Rose had been married 69 years.

At the age of 95, McCoubrey learned to use the computer; he surfed the Internet and visited senior chat rooms, where he enjoyed letting people believe he was only 65, Beth Salveson said.

"He did not resist change — he embraced change, and he enjoyed new technology," she said. "The Internet, he very much enjoyed that, and it allowed him to interact with people and help keep him vital."

"Everybody gravitated to him," Beth Salveson continued. "He was something of a raconteur because he liked to tell stories." He did that to the end." She said.

At 110, he became a "supercentenarian," his age verified by the Gerontology Research Group (GRG). Upon the death of the previous oldest man in the world in Japan on

June 12, 2013, McCoubrey was the oldest man in the world whose documentation had been verified by the group, according to Robert Young, senior database administrator for GRG and a senior consultant for gerontology for Guinness World Records.

"Ninety percent of supercentenarians are women. Of the 56 oldest people in the world, 54 are women," Young said following McCoubrey's death.

OVER THE LIPS ...

Newfoundland Screech is a type of specific rum sold in Newfoundland. It has 40 per cent of alcohol by volume.

The term "screech" is a colloquial term that has been used to describe almost any cheap, high alcohol spirit, including moonshine. The term is used in the brand name for this mid-priced rum to associate the brand with this tradition.

Newfoundland Screech is sold in liquor stores both in and outside of Newfoundland and is blended and bottled by the Newfoundland and Labrador Liquor Corporation (NLC), which, unlike their counterparts in other provinces, NLC has retained its bottling business. The spirit is widely available in Canada and is also distributed in the New England States (Maine, New Hampshire, and Vermont) of the United States.

Screech-in

Newfoundland Screech is used in a traditional Newfoundland ceremony known as the "screech-in."

The "screech-in" is an optional ceremony performed on non-Newfoundlanders (known to Newfoundlanders as a "come from away" or "mainlander") involving a shot of screech, a short recitation and the kissing of a cod. It is often performed either in homes or more commonly in town pubs. Screech-ins also take place aboard tourist boat excursions.

The general process of a screech-in varies from pub to pub and community to community, though it often begins with the leader of the ceremony introducing themselves and asking those present if they'd like to become a Newfoundlander.

The proper response, of course, would be a hearty "Yes b'y!"

Participants are asked to introduce themselves and tell where they come from, often interrupted by commentary by the ceremony leader, jokingly poking fun at their accent or hometown.

Each holding their shot of Screech, they are then asked "Are ye a screecher?" and are taught the proper response, "'Deed I is, me ol' cock! And long may yer big jib draw!"

Translated, it means, "Yes I am, my old friend, and may your sails always catch wind."

A cod fish — or any other fish ugly enough to suitably replace the cod — is then held up to lip-level of each participant, who then bestows the fish with a kiss. Frozen fish are used most commonly in the screech-ins, which take place on George St., though occasionally a fresher specimen, if available, will be used. Some pubs will also award certificates to those who have become an honorary Newfie once the screech-in is complete.

Some screech-in traditions vary in both the order of events, as well as the necessary requirements. Some ceremonies require that the screech-ee eat a piece of "Newfie steak" (a slice of baloney) or kiss a rubber puffin's rear end. Some are also asked to stand in a bucket of salt water throughout the ceremony or that they wear the Sou'wester during the recitation and the drinking of the shot.

For group screech-ins, the shots and recitations are generally all done at once. In all cases, no matter what, only a native Newfoundlander can officiate a proper screech-in.

LADIES FIRST

Sheila NaGiera, According to legend, Sheila NaGiera was the first European woman to settle in Newfoundland when she and her husband Gilbert Pike made the Island their home in 1611.

Gilbert was a fisherman and former pirate while Sheila — said to be a princess — was a member of a wealthy Irish family. It has been suggested that NaGeira may be an epithet meaning *the beautiful*, and that Sheila's actual last name was O'Connor, making her the daughter of a claimant to the Irish throne of Connacht.

As the story goes, in 1602, Sheila was a young Irish noblewoman on her return trip sailing from France, where she had been studying in a French convent run by her aunt, an abbess. She was captured by a Dutch privateer in the English Channel, and subsequently rescued by Peter Easton, an English privateer loyal to Queen Elizabeth I.

At the time, Easton's fleet was on its way to Newfoundland to protect the English fishing fleet there. Easton took his rescued prisoners to Newfoundland with him, including Sheila. While a passenger aboard Easton's vessel, it is said she fell in love with his lieutenant, Gilbert Pike and they eventually married.

By this time, Pike had left Easton's employ and the couple settled in a place called Mosquito Cove, known today as Bristol's Hope. In 1611, they moved to nearby Carbonear to escape the return of Easton, who by that time became a much-feared pirate under the reign of James I.

The legend of Sheila NaGeira also has it that she was the first European woman to give birth in Newfoundland and quite possibly North America (although Virginia Dare is reported to have been born in the Roanoke Colony, North Carolina, in 1587, and the Vinland Sagas record the birth of Snorri Thorfinnsson to Icelandic parents around the year 1005 in Vinland, in the Viking settlement at L'Anse aux Meadows).

Adding to the legend, Sheila NaGeira is sometimes claimed to have been the Island's first schoolteacher, midwife and herbal doctor. The mythology of Shelia NaGeira seems to have first been recorded in print at the beginning of the twentieth Century, as there is no mention of her in any of the histories of the Island or its folk beliefs prior to that. It is possible a local legend pre-dates that, but no evidence has been found to date.

The official record for a European child born in Newfoundland was on March 27, 1613 to a Nicholas Guy and his wife, whose name was not recorded. There are no historical records of a Sheila NaGeira existing, let alone having given birth, or being married to a Gilbert Pike. In 1982, the Canadian Conservation Institute confirmed that the alleged burial place for Sheila showed a crumbling stone of a John Pike, but there was no mention of a Sheila.

Lady Helena E. Squires, Lady Helena E. Squires (Strong) and her twin sister were born in Little Bay Islands, Newfoundland in 1879. The Strong sisters were educated at a boarding school at the St. John's Methodist College and later at Mount Allison University, where she trained to be a teacher.

The wife of Sir Richard Anderson Squires, the Prime Minister of the province, Lady Helena eventually became the first woman to stand for and win a seat in the Newfoundland and Labrador (formerly Newfoundland) House of Assembly, in the 1930 by-election as the Member for the District of Lewisporte. She lost her seat in 1932. The mother of seven children, Lady Helena was also a social activist who worked to found a teacher's school and a maternity hospital.

One of her sons, named after her husband, Richard Anderson Squires, served with Lord Strathcona's Horse regiment in the Canadian army during the Second World War. He was killed on June 17, 1942 at Headley Downs, England. The 31-year-old Lieutenant had been riding on the outside of his tank during manoeuvres in order to direct his driver when the tank lurched, throwing him forward and under the track of the moving tank.

When Newfoundland joined Confederation in 1949, Lady Squires was elected the first president of the provincial Liberal Association, a position she held until 1958. Helena died in 1959 at her retirement home in Toronto.

Edith Weeks Hooper, Edith Weeks Hooper was the first Newfoundland born woman to become a medical doctor and the first female doctor to practice in the province. She graduated from the University of Toronto Medical School in 1906.

Kathleen "Kathy" Dunderdale, Born in February 1952 in Burin, she served as the tenth Premier of Newfoundland and Labrador and was in office from December 3, 2010, to January 24, 2014. Before entering politics she worked in the fields of community development, communications, fisheries and social work. Her first foray into politics was as a member of the Burin town council, where she served as deputy mayor.

In the 2003 general election, Dunderdale was elected as Member of the House of Assembly for the riding of Virginia Waters. She was re-elected in the 2007 and 2011 general elections and resigned her post on February 28, 2014.

Dunderdale served in the cabinets of Danny Williams, holding the portfolios of Innovation, Trade and Rural Development, Natural Resources and Deputy Premier, where she developed a reputation as one of the most high-profile members of Williams' cabinets.

Dunderdale became premier upon the resignation of Williams and after becoming the PC leader she led the party to victory in the October 2011 election. Dunderdale was the first female premier in the province's history and the sixth woman to serve as a premier in the history of Canada.

FLYING INTO THE HISTORY BOOKS

Amelia Mary Earhart, who was born on July 24, 1897, was an American aviation pioneer and author. She became the first female aviator to fly solo across the Atlantic Ocean and also claimed the honour of being the first woman to fly a plane in Newfoundland.

As trans-Atlantic aviation became more popular in the 1920s and 1930s, many aviation pioneers — among them Earhart — chose to make their crossing from the airfield in Harbour Grace, Newfoundland due to its proximity to continental Europe.

Altogether, some twenty flights left Harbour Grace from 1927 to 1936 in their attempts to cross the Atlantic. The first civilian airstrip at Harbour Grace, built in

1927, is the oldest surviving operational airstrip in Canada and was the place of origin for Amelia Earhart's successful 1932 solo flight across the Atlantic.

In 1928, Earhart was accompanied by William S. Stultz and Lew Cordon when they took off from Trepassey, Newfoundland, in their bid to cross the Atlantic non-stop by hydroplane. On that occasion, she became the first woman to cross the Atlantic by plane, but she was far from done.

At the age of 34, Earhart set off from Harbour Grace, Newfoundland in her single engine Lockheed Vega 5B at 7:20 p.m. on May 20, 1932, and flew into the sunset. She carried with her a copy of the *Telegraph-Journal*, given to her by journalist Stuart Trueman, intended to confirm the date of the flight. She also took along a thermos bottle of soup and a can of tomato juice.

After a challenging flight that lasted 14 hours and 56 minutes, during which she contended with strong northerly winds, icy conditions and mechanical problems, Earhart landed in a cow field at Londonderry, Northern Ireland.

It was a hazardous flight due to the fact that her altimeter wasn't working, which meant she didn't know how high she was above the ocean. In the end, though, she arrived safely though, albeit, a little off course. She had intended to fly to Paris to emulate Charles Lindbergh's solo flight, but instead ended up in a pasture at Culmore.

The landing was witnessed by Cecil King and T. Sawyer. When a farm hand asked, "Have you flown far?" Earhart replied, "From America." The site now is the home of a small museum, the Amelia Earhart Centre.

Earhart received the U.S. Distinguished Flying Cross for setting this record. She set many other records, wrote best-selling books about her flying experiences and was instrumental in the formation of the Ninety-Nines, an organization for female pilots.

Earhart joined the faculty of the Purdue University aviation department in 1935 as a visiting faculty member to counsel women on careers, and helped inspire others with her love for aviation. She was also a member of the National Woman's Party, and an early supporter of the Equal Rights Amendment.

During an attempt to make a circumnavigational flight of the globe in 1937 in a Purdue-funded Lockheed Model 10 Electra, Earhart disappeared on July 2 over the central Pacific Ocean near Howland Island.

Whatever happened to Amelia Earhart was a mystery, and fascination with her life, career and disappearance continues to this day.

Statues of a Labrador Retriever and a Newfoundland dog located in Harborside Park in St. John's. Both breeds originated in Newfoundland. The one and one half life-size sculptures made from cast bronze over a steel framework are from artist Luben Boykov and were completed in 2003.

GONE TO THE DOGS

Newfoundland and Labrador has the distinction of being the only Canadian province that can claim two native dog breeds — the Newfoundland and the Labrador retriever.

The Newfoundland

The Newfoundland was bred to be a working dog. Newfoundlands are large in size and can be black, brown, white and black gray. However, in Canada, the country of their origin, the only correct colours are black (including black with white markings) and white and black.

Originally, the dogs were bred and used as a working dog for fishermen. They are well known for their even temperament and stoic nature. They are also known for their giant size, intelligence, tremendous strength, calm dispositions and loyalty.

The Newfoundland's extremely large bones give it mass, while its large musculature gives it the power it needs to take on rough ocean waves and powerful tides. They excel at water rescue and lifesaving because of their muscular build, thick double coat, webbed feet, and innate swimming abilities. These dogs have great lung capacity for swimming extremely long distances, and a thick, oily and waterproof double coat, which protects them from the chill of icy waters.

In the water, the dog's massive webbed paws give it maximum propulsion. The swimming stroke is not an ordinary dog paddle. Unlike other dogs, the Newfoundland moves its limbs in a down-and-out motion. This gives it more power with every stroke.

Males in this breed normally weigh 60–70 kg (130–150 lb), and females 45–55 kg (99–121 lb). The largest on record weighed 120 kg (260 lb) and measured over 1.8 m (6 ft) from nose to tail. They may grow up to 56–76 cm (22–30 in) tall at the shoulder.

Because of its breeding, the Newfoundland dog is as much at home in the water as on dry land. There are many stories throughout the province's history of brave Newfoundlands which have rescued men and women from watery graves, stories of shipwrecks made less terrible by dogs which carried life lines to stricken vessels, of children who have fallen into deep water and have been brought safely ashore by Newfoundlands, and of dogs whose work was less spectacular but equally valuable as they helped their fishermen owners with their heavy nets and preformed other tasks necessary to their occupations.

Labrador Retrievers

So that's the Newfoundland dog, but what of its canine cousin, the Labrador retriever?

Also known as the Labrador, the Labrador retriever is one of the most popular breeds of dog in the United Kingdom and the United States.

The Labrador has a dense, short coat that repels water and provides great resistance to the cold and water. Labradors come in three colours — black, yellow and chocolate. Black is the most well-known colour and it is dominant in Labradors. Black was also the colour commonly preferred and bred for, up until more recent times.

Used far and wide as disability assistance dogs in many countries, Labradors are frequently trained to aid the blind and those who have autism, to act as therapy dogs and perform screening and detection work for law enforcement and other official agencies. They are also prized as sporting and hunting dogs.

A history of the Labrador retriever found on a website for Lorken Farms in Fremont, WI, says the Labrador retriever is considered a "flushing" dog that will retrieve the game for the hunter once down. They are generally used to hunt both upland game birds and waterfowl. More recently, some have worked on perfecting a pointing characteristic with Labradors. Labradors have also come to be one of the favourite family house pets in North America today due to their wonderful personality, gentle disposition and loyalty.

Labrador Retrievers were recognized in England as a Kennel Club breed in 1903 and first registered by the American Kennel Club in the United States in 1917. Labradors were originally called a St. John's Dog or lesser Newfoundland dog. The breed was first reported in Newfoundland in the 1700s and imported to England in the early 1800s.

The Labrador's exact origin is unknown but some speculate the Greater Newfoundland dog or the French St. Hubert's dog is part of the cross that made the St. John's dog.

In 1887, the Earl of Malmesbury first coined the name Labrador in a letter he wrote, referring to them as his Labrador Dogs.

Fisherman in Newfoundland used the St. John's dog to retrieve fish that had fallen off their hooks as well to help haul in fishing lines through the water. The dogs were considered "workaholics" and enjoyed the retrieving tasks given in the fishing environment. This breed was very eager to please and their retrieving abilities made them ideal as hunting companions and sporting dogs.

It was said that the dogs would work long hours with the fisherman in the cold waters, then be brought home to play with the fisherman's children. The wonderful temperament of the Labrador retriever is documented back to its early days in England and has made them ideal family pets as well as accomplished sporting dogs.

Labradors almost became extinct a few times and the St. John's dogs that Labs came from are now extinct in Newfoundland. It was only through some events and efforts of some key people that the breed survived.

Newfoundland pony.

A RARE BREED, INDEED

Newfoundland and Labrador is the only Canadian province to have its own horse. The Newfoundland pony has been around for generations and has been part of the landscape in communities all over the province.

According to information found on the Newfoundland Pony Society's website, the pony owes its origins to the earliest settlers who brought a variety of mountain and moorland ponies from Europe to the province. They were considered an essential ingredient in taming the rugged land and in meeting the many challenges of survival.

"The Newfoundland pony, as we know it today, is a distinct landrace breed that evolved over time from the interbreeding of these original herds of ponies, that when they were not being worked, were allowed to run wild over the provincial landscape," the society says. "And so this hardy, gentle, loyal and lovable pony is a true example of a landrace animal that bred and evolved naturally without any human interference until modern times."

This unique and wonderful animal has been recently listed as Critically Endangered by Rare Breeds Canada, The Livestock Conservancy, and Equus Survival Trust. According to the society's website, one of the primary roles of the Society under provincial government legislation is to conserve, protect and preserve the pony for future generations.

"We welcome your help and support in ensuring that this pony with its wonderful history has a bright future," the society says. "It is known for its capacity to survive and thrive but at this time it needs all the help we can muster."

FIVE FAST FACTS

1 With seven in a 24-hour-period, Daniels Harbour is the town with the most lightning storms in a single day.

2 In 2004, the Canadian Oxford English Dictionary added the word "Wreckhouse Winds" to its word catalogue. The word is defined as, extremely strong winds, which blow across Cape Ray from the Long Range Mountains in Newfoundland.

3 Icebergs, which "calve" (or sheer off) from glaciers, are made of compressed snow. They are fresh — not salt — water.

4 According to SOS Canada, the largest wave ever recorded anywhere in the world was in Newfoundland and Labrador waters. The record-setting 30m wave, generated by Hurricane Luis in 1995, slammed against the luxury liner Queens Elizabeth II as it sailed off the southern coast of Newfoundland.

5 The International Ice Patrol (IIP) was created in 1912 after the Titanic collided with a North Atlantic iceberg. This organization compiles charts and broadcasts ice bulletins to warn sailors of conditions. It is financed by 17 nations around the world.

GEOGRAPHY/WEATHER

THE LAY OF THE LAND

Newfoundland and Labrador is the most easterly province in Canada. It is made up of Newfoundland (Island) and Labrador (mainland). The two geographical divisions are separated by the Strait of Belle Isle. The province also includes over seven thousand small Islands.

Labrador is the easternmost part of the Canadian Shield, a vast area of ancient metamorphic rock comprising much of northeastern North America. Colliding tectonic plates have shaped much of the geology of Newfoundland. Gros Morne National Park has a reputation of being an outstanding example of tectonics at work, and as such has been designated a World Heritage Site.

GEOGRAPHICAL STATS

    Total coastline, 17,542 km (10,900 mi)

    Land borders, Quebec and Nunavut

    Highest point, Mount Caubvick at 1,652 metres (5,420 ft)

    Lowest point, Atlantic Ocean at 0 m

    Longest river, Churchill River at 856 km (532 mi)

    Largest inland body of water, Smallwood Reservoir at 31,153 km^2 (12,028 sq. mi)

    Climate, Temperate to Arctic

    Terrain, Mountains, subarctic, arctic

Natural resources, iron ore, nickel, zinc, copper, gold, silver, fish, timber, petroleum, hydropower

Cape Spear Lighthouse is the most easterly point in North America and is a national historic site.

THE FURTHEST EAST YOU CAN GO

Cape Spear, located on the Avalon Peninsula near St. John's, is the easternmost point in Canada. The Portuguese named the location "Cabo da Esperança" which means "cape of hope." It subsequently became "Cap d'Espoir" in French and finally "Cape Spear."

Cape Spear Lighthouse, which began operations in September 1836, is the oldest surviving lighthouse in Newfoundland and the location has been designated a National Historic Site. The original Cape Spear lighthouse was the second lighthouse built in Newfoundland. The first was built in 1810 at Fort Amherst, at the entrance to St. John's Harbour.

In 1832, the first legislative assembly for the colony created a lighthouse board. Cape Spear was chosen as the site for a new lighthouse because it was on the rocky eastern coast near the entrance to St. John's Harbour.

A foghorn was added in 1878. The first light used at Cape Spear had already been used since 1815 at a lighthouse at Inchkeith on the east coast of Scotland. Because of its proximity to convoy routes during the Second World War, a gun battery was installed at Cape Spear to defend the entrance to St. John's harbour. Barracks and underground passages leading to the bunkers were built for the use of troops stationed there.

THE LEWIS HILLS

The Long Range Mountains on Newfoundland's west coast are the northeasternmost extension of the Appalachian Mountains. The Lewis Hills is a section of the Long Range Mountains along the Gulf of St. Lawrence.

An ophiolite and Peridotite complex, the Lewis Hills is the southernmost of four such complexes located within the Humber Arm Allochthon, a world-renowned geological area. It is located in an area stretching between the town of Stephenville in the south and the city of Corner Brook in the north.

THE LONG RANGE MOUNTAINS

The Long Range Mountains are a series of mountains along the west coast of Newfoundland. They also form the northernmost section of the Appalachian chain on the eastern seaboard of North America.

The 10 highest peaks of the Long Range Mountains are:
1. The Cabox, 814 m (2,671 ft)
2. Gros Morne, 807 m (2,644 ft)
3. Blue Mountain, 800 m (2,625 ft)
4. Big Level, 795 m (2,608 ft)
5. Round Hill, 763 m (2,653 ft)
6. Rocky Harbour Hill, 756 m (2,480 ft)
7. Mount Saint Gregory, 686 m (2,251 ft)
8. Gros Paté, 673 m (2,208 ft)
9. Big Hill, 659 m (2,162 ft)
10. Old Crow, 649 m (2,129 ft)

LET IT SNOW, LET IT SNOW, LET IT SNOW

The town of Woody Point, Newfoundland, tallies the highest snowfall measurements in Canada. It is located on Bonne Bay of Newfoundland's west coast, next to Gros Morne National Park. Over a typical winter, Woody Point racks up 638 centimeters, nearly 21 feet of snow that lands in just 89 days.

St. Anthony, Newfoundland, which, on average, tallies 543.7 centimeters (214.0 inches) in 103 days, and Main Brook, Newfoundland, with accumulations totaling 515.0 centimeters (202.8 inches) in 51 days, rank fifth and sixth respectively on the list of Canada's snowiest places.

A car is buried in snow following a massive winter blizzard in St. John's.

ONE FOR THE RECORD BOOKS

The biggest one-day snowfall to ever hit Newfoundland and Labrador was the blizzard of February 5, 1988 that dropped 105.0 centimeters (41.3 inches) on the community of Main Brook.

The blizzard of January 6, 1988, that left 103.4 centimeters (40.7 inches) on Nain holds the record for the second biggest snow dump in one day, while the storm of February 17, 1943, that deposited 101.6 centimetres (40.0 inches) on Colient holds the record for the third biggest snowfall in one day.

The Newfoundland communities that report at least 1 cm (0.4 inches) deep snow on the ground are Churchill Falls (221 days), Makkovik (210 days), Nain (205 days) and Wabush Lake (202 days).

THE ANSWER IS BLOWING IN THE WIND

Canada is usually only hit with weak storms, due to the generally cool waters immediately offshore. However, some hurricanes can strike the area full force as the warm Gulf Stream extends fairly close to Atlantic Canada.

Many tropical storms and hurricanes struck Canada before the 1900s. The most damaging one struck Newfoundland in September 1775, killing thousands. Following is a list of hurricanes that affected Newfoundland and Labrador prior to its entry into Canada in 1949 and in the years since then.

- September 9, 1775. The Newfoundland Hurricane of 1775 killed over 4,000 people in Newfoundland. Not only is it the earliest recorded Canadian hurricane, it is also by far the deadliest on record.
- September 23–24, 1866. A hurricane hit Newfoundland after weakening from a category 2.
- September 8, 1891. A hurricane struck both Nova Scotia and Newfoundland as a category 1.
- August 18, 1893. A hurricane struck Newfoundland with 90 mph (145 km/h) winds.
- October 18, 1939. After a long respite from hurricanes in Newfoundland, a hurricane struck the Island as a category 1. No one died, but considerable damage was done to trees, boats and buildings.
- September 29, 1958. Hurricane Helene struck Newfoundland as a hurricane, destroying a 50-metre (160 foot) wharf carrying many lobsters out to sea.

- August 7–8, 1988. Tropical Storm Alberto, the furthest north forming tropical storm ever recorded in the Atlantic, struck the Maritimes and became extra-tropical over Newfoundland. Alberto was the first storm with a masculine name to directly strike Canada.
- September 11, 1995. Hurricane Luis, after raging through the Leeward Islands, turned towards Newfoundland on September 8. The Canadian Hurricane Centre issued bulletins on the powerful hurricane as it neared the province. Luis struck a sparsely populated area in eastern Newfoundland on September 11, dropping 2 to 4 inches (60–120 mm) of rain in the Avalon Peninsula without causing much damage. One person was reported killed in Canada from Luis.
- October 20, 2000. Hurricane Michael struck Harbour Breton as a category 1 hurricane. A peak gust was recorded of nearly 107 mph (171 km/h), as well as a peak wave height of over 55 feet (16.7 m). Overall, however, damage by Michael was light.
- September 17, 2005. Hurricane Ophelia, after stalling for several days off the coast of the southeastern states, raced up the Atlantic coast. On September 17, Ophelia became extra-tropical and moved parallel to the Nova Scotian coast, never making landfall. Ophelia later struck Newfoundland. Although strong winds were forecast, they did not occur and overall damage was less than expected. One indirect death was reported from Ophelia in Canada.
- September 21, 2010. Hurricane Igor struck Cape Race as a large category 1 hurricane, resulting in major flooding and widespread power outages. Many communities were forced to declare a state of emergency, and some evacuated completely as the storm approached. Igor was unusual in that it picked up strength during its final approach despite being over cool water. As the storm made landfall near Cape Race, maximum sustained winds were estimated to be at least 120 km/h (80 mph), but gusts up to 170 km/h (105 mph) were reported. Hurricane Igor produced hurricane conditions throughout the Avalon Peninsula and tropical storm conditions over the remainder of the Island. Media outlets have stated that Igor was the worst hurricane to hit Newfoundland in a century.
- September 16, 2011. Hurricane Maria made landfall near the Avalon Peninsula of Newfoundland. Due to Maria's rapid forward speed (90+ km/h), rainfall totals were kept to a minimum and strong winds remained offshore, confined to the eastern semi-circle. As a result, little damage occurred.
- September 11, 2012. Hurricane Leslie made landfall on the Burin Peninsula of Newfoundland as a hurricane-strength post-tropical cyclone. Leslie's track put the Avalon Peninsula in the right-front quadrant, resulting in hurricane-force winds, widespread power outages, and structural damage.

OUTPORT REPORT

Newfoundland outports were small, isolated coastal fishing communities located throughout the Island that represented some of the earliest European settlements in Canada. In the mid-20th Century, however, steps were taken to dismantle these centuries-old villages and resettle the citizens elsewhere.

In 1954, the Provincial government began to relocate outport residents to areas called "growth centres" that were situated in more strategic locations. In 1965, the Federal Government became a partner in the scheme, believing that relocated Newfoundlanders would earn better livelihoods and have easier access to social services if they lived in less removed communities.

Cash payments in return for compliance proved a powerful incentive to poor fishers who struggled to survive, and by 1975, a total of 250 outports across the province had been abandoned. Almost 45,000 people, roughly 10 per cent of Newfoundland's population, were resettled.

In the end, the results of resettlement were mixed, and by the late 1970s, critics were calling resettlement a failure. Many relocated families were unable to secure fishing licenses in growth centres, and unemployment among the resettled was high.

With their prospects bleak, some former outport residents ultimately returned to abandoned villages, but the majority did not. Others kept and still keep, summerhouses in abandoned outports. Regardless, though, the resettlement project was deemed a failure, having destroyed communities that had been in existence for hundreds of years.

RAWLINS CROSS

The famed Newfoundland landmark, located in the historic city of St. John's, is formed by the intersection of Prescott Street, Monkstown and Military Roads.

Military Road, built in 1773, was one of the first roads in this area that joined Fort William with Fort Townsend. Monkstown Road was built in the early 19th Century and Prescott Street around 1840. The area where all three came together became to be known as Rawlins Cross, named after local grocer Patrick Rawlins.

Rawlins Cross has been home to many businesses over the years. One of the most noteworthy was O'Mara-Martin Drugs that was established in 1892. In 1895, W.J. Murphy's grocery also established a presence there.

Rawlins Cross is the site of the city's first traffic light. When it was first installed and for many years, a police constable, stationed at the intersection, manually operated it. A commemorative plaque for the St. John's Electric Light Company is located at Rawlins Cross, although the business was established on nearby Flavin Street in 1885.

A distinct feature of this area is the difference in the style of houses on either side of the intersection. One side has large luxury homes that once belonged to fish merchants, while on the other side, and closer to downtown, small row houses are located, accentuating the great economic and social divide. In the late 19th and early 20th centuries, these row houses belonged to poor fishermen, who worked for the merchants on the opposing side of the intersection.

The popular Newfoundland Irish band, Rawlins Cross, takes its name from this St. John's landmark.

ROUND OR FLAT?

Brimstone Head on Fogo Island is a piece of rocky landscape that the Flat Earth Society believes to be one of the four corners of the Earth.

Brimstone Head is one of the four corners of the earth according to the satirical Canadian Flat Earth Society. Where is Brimstone Head? Well, the rocky promontory is located on Fogo Island, 15 kilometers off the northeast coast of Newfoundland.

Where are the four corners of the earth? A sign on the Brimstone Trail summit claims that they are at Papua New Guinea, the Bermuda Triangle, the Greek Island of Hydra, as well as Fogo, Newfoundland.

Fogo residents are happy that the Flat Earth Society's claim draws tourists to climb Brimstone Head. Some visitors travel to Fogo Island on the ferry from Farewell, on the mainland, to Stag Harbour. (The ferry crossing time is 40 minutes.) They then drive along route 333 to the community of Fogo.

Brimstone Head is actually a volcanic landmark and from a distance, the rounded promontory resembles an upside-down cupcake dominating the community. The area around Fogo is comprised of very hard volcanic rock, created 420 million years ago in a dramatic Pompeii-like explosion.

A sign at the summit of Brimstone Head advises, "Warning. You are nearing the edge of the flat earth. One false step could be your last. Number of people lost to date, 0."

The distance between Brimstone Head to Toronto is 2,088 kilometers. Even more interesting, is the fact that the distance between Fogo, Newfoundland, and London, England, (3,906 kilometers) is far closer than Fogo Island to Vancouver (4,925 kilometers).

So what is the Flat Earthy Society?

According to its website, "The Mission of the mission of the Flat Earth Society is to promote and initiate the discussion of Flat Earth theory as well as archive Flat Earth literature."

FIVE FAST FACTS

1 On January 1, 1977, barometers at St. Anthony recorded the lowest sea-level pressure ever in Canada. The reading was 94.02 kpa.

2 Between 1750 and 1791, there were twenty trials for murder in Newfoundland.

3 Canada's first Subway restaurant opened in June 1986 in the city of St. John's.

4 The first baseball games in St. John's (1929) were played indoors at Prince's Rink.

5 Mary Ewing Outerbridge introduced lawn tennis to North America in 1874. The Newfoundlander introduced it to her brother in Staten Island after she had seen it played in Bermuda.

HISTORICALLY SPEAKING

THE BEOTHUK

One of the most tragic stories in Newfoundland and Labrador's history is the loss of an entire Aboriginal people, the Beothuk. A creation story attributed to the Beothuk tells of how they sprang from an arrow stuck in the ground.

It is doubtful that early Beothuk storytellers could possibly have foretold their demise. By 1829, there were no Beothuk left in Newfoundland, though residents have stories of half-blood ancestors.

As part of the Algonkian family, it is estimated the Beothuk probably numbered around 700 people at the time of the first European contact. The Beothuk had an animistic worldview — they believed that animate and inanimate objects had spiritual dimensions. For the Beothuk, the most important spirits were the sun and the moon.

European fishers who encountered the Beothuk in the 16th Century commented on their use of ochre, a red pigment, to colour their skin. In subsequent years, the term "Red Indian" was applied to many First Peoples in North America, even when it did not apply.

Red ochre had important cultural meanings for the Beothuk. They covered their bodies, clothes, weapons, utensils, canoes and even their infants with the pigments to symbolize their tribal identity. The name "Beothuk" comes from the people's own name for themselves — "Beathook" and "Behathook," which translates as "Red Indian."

Early European settlement in Newfoundland was largely migratory with fishers remaining just for the fishing season. Instead of trading with the Europeans, the Beothuk picked up metal scraps they had left behind, fashioning them into a wide range of tools, such as harpoon blades, awls and arrowheads.

Because the Beothuk could obtain metal this way, while other continental Aboriginals had to trade for it, they had no need to interact with fishers. They took materials that were apparently abandoned. The fishing crews that returned each year, however, saw it as theft.

Beginning of the end

The beginning of the end arrived for the Beothuk was when European settlement became permanent. The Beothuk retreated to the interior, avoiding the Europeans as much as possible. For a time, Newfoundland's size and rich resources meant there were buffer zones between the Beothuk and the Europeans, but as settlement increased, they began to disappear.

With increased European settlements, the Beothuk faced starvation. They lost access to the coastal resources on which they relied, and faced competition for the resources they could reach. It became more and more difficult for them to avoid Europeans and violence escalated. As with Aboriginal people elsewhere, the Beothuk also became sickened by European diseases to which they had little immunity. Meanwhile, fishers and trappers wanted restitution for Beothuk pilfering of their fishing stations, and violent clashes resulted in Beothuks being felled by settlers' bullets.

By 1800, European settlers had still not established a friendly relationship with the shrinking population of Beothuk. Motivated by humanitarian interests and by a desire to institute trade, the English launched a concerted campaign to find and befriend the Beothuk. Rewards were offered to anyone who brought a living Beothuk to St. John's. The plan was to treat the hostage kindly, shower him or her with presents, and then return the captive to the Beothuk, thus demonstrating kindness and goodwill.

In 1811, an English expedition sent by Governor John Duckworth met with Beothuk at Red Indian Lake, where they shared a meal. Pleased by the peaceful exchange, expedition leader Lt. David Buchanan left two of his men with the Beothuk and returned to his camp to fetch presents for his hosts. The Beothuk, probably fearing Buchanan would return with more men and take them hostage, killed the two Englishmen and returned to the woods.

Eight years after the killings at Red Indian Lake, John Peyton, Jr., angry that a boat loaded with the fishing equipment had been set adrift by the Beothuk, went after the perpetrators. When he came across a Beothuk camp, he kidnapped Demasduit, a new mother too weak to escape. When Demasduit's husband, Nonosabasut, tried to rescue his wife and child, he was killed.

Mary March

Dubbed "Mary March" by her captors (for the month in which she was taken), Demasduit was taken to Twillingate where she lived with the Reverend John Leigh. Her infant child died two days after her capture. In mere months, her body wracked with tuberculosis, Demaduit followed her husband and child to the grave. In

January 1820, her body was returned to the Beothuk, left on the spot from which had been captured.

A number of Beothuk witnessed the murder of Nonosabasut, including his young niece, Shanawdithit. Several years later, following the very hard winter of 1823-24, Shanawdithit, her mother and her sister, all sick and near starvation, threw themselves on the mercy of fur trappers. Shortly thereafter, Shanawdithit's mother and sister died.

Shanawdithit was placed in the home of the local magistrate, John Peyton, Jr. — the same man that had captured Demasduit. Shanawdithit was treated kindly and she lived in Peyton's household for five years. A group of concerned citizens sponsored her to visit St. John's, where she was interviewed by William Cormack, the philanthropist president of the Beothuk Institute, an organization mandated to preserve the Beothuk.

Shanawdithit provided Cormack with valuable information about her people and their culture. A gifted artist, her sketches remain one of the most important first-hand sources of knowledge about the Beothuk.

Shanawdithit lived in St. John's for five years. By 1829, she was in very poor health and in June she died of tuberculosis at the age of 28. Unlike Demaduit, Shanawdithit had no family to whom she could be returned so she was buried in a grave in St. John's. Shanawdithit left a priceless legacy. Virtually everything that is known about Beothuk culture, as it existed in the early 19th Century, came from her.

THE INUIT OF LABRADOR

An Arctic people, the Inuit of Labrador now have their own ethnic regional government in the northern part of the province. Nunatsiavut (meaning "beautiful land") was officially created on December 1, 2005, following years of land-claims negotiations. It encompasses 72,500 square kilometers of land.

They speak a language called Inuktitut and in that language "Inuit" means "the people."

Before encountering Europeans, the Inuit lived by hunting and fishing. On land, caribou was their most important food supply, while the sea offered a harvest of seals to whales and cod to salmon throughout the year.

The Inuit, like many First Peoples, believe in the power of shamans or "angakut." Spirit helpers, called "Torngat," aid the shamans. The Inuit believe that all prominent geographic forms have a spiritual counterpart. The environment teems with spirits who the Inuit have to placate or guard against. For example, to hear the favour of the spirits and ensure a successful hunt, they must place new seal skins on their kayaks, observe a taboo against chopping wood, refrain from sewing and from eating berries, and avoid the use of artificial light.

The most spiritual of Inuit sites is Torngait, on the northern Labrador coast. There, they believe that the Great Spirit Torngarsoak, who controls the life of all sea animals, lives in the form of a giant polar bear. Torngait is dangerous and the Inuit take precautions when they travel there.

Dwellings

The Inuit had three types of traditional dwellings in which they lived. In summer, they lived in conical tents made of skins. On hunting trips, they built temporary snow homes. In winter, semi-permanent homes of stone and sod were dug into the ground for insulation. The Inuit burned seal oil for light and heat.

Many Inuit still live off the land, hunting, fishing and trapping when they can, though they may live in established communities in the winter. They also find employment in the mines of Labrador and in other non-traditional jobs.

Today, most Labrador Inuit live in five communities that are recognized by the federal Department of Indian and Northern Development — Nain, Hopedale, Makkovik, Postville and Rigolet.

In all, four percent of Canadian Inuit live in Labrador. It is estimated there are roughly 6,265 Inuit in the province as a whole with 2,325 in Nunatsiavut and 680 in St. John's.

THE INNU

Before encountering Europeans, the Innu migrated seasonally to take advantage of the best hunting. They had a meat-rich diet, with caribou being an important staple. The taking of a caribou was often celebrated with a special feast called Mokushan.

The Innu believe they originated in Tshishtashkamuk, a spirit world that, like their physical world, contains vegetation, water and mountains. They believe they were forced out of this world by a flood, crossing a land bridge into the real world they now inhabit.

The Innu see their environment as a world where spirits exist and influence life. Animals have spirits and each species is ruled over by an "animal master," those of caribou and sea animals being most powerful. Other inhabitants of the spirit world included giants, weather spirits and cannibals.

An important Innu atanukana, or creation story, involves Caribou Man and explains the origin of the caribou. According to the story, an Innu man went to live with a herd of caribou. When he married a female caribou, he was transformed into one of the animals and became the Caribou Master. He provides all Innu with caribou.

Kushapatshikan, the shaking tent ritual, is one of the most important Innu traditions. It allows Innu hunters to ensure success by communicating with Caribou Man and other animal masters. During this séance-like ritual, a shaman enters a conical tent, which allows him contact with the spirit world.

Sometimes the shaman has to battle against spirits or the souls of other Innu groups. During this struggle the tent may shake furiously, greatly amusing observers, but shaking tent can be dangerous and those without sufficient powers, accumulated by years of hunting, may even be killed.

Failed Relocation

In 1967, the federal government relocated 100 Mushuau Innu to the Island community of Davis Inlet, a community six kilometers away from their former village with a better harbor. In Utshimassitsm, or the "place of the boss," the once mobile new occupants were supposed to ease into an Ottawa-funded life of permanent and modern fixed settlement.

Sadly, the hope that was in the air on moving day faded. The bored and uprooted people of Davis Inlet were crammed into small houses that lacked basic amenities such as running water and electricity. In a community affected by high levels of unemployment, alcoholism became a serious social problem. In the 1990s, national evening newscasts brought the Davis Inlet truth to Canadians who watched children, high on solvents, proclaim they want to die.

As international Native rights organizations called the Davis Inlet inhabitants "the most suicide-ridden people of the world" and blamed Ottawa for their fate. Spurred by the disheartening events, Innu elders, desperate to renew their community advocated moving again, this time to a traditional Innu gathering place near the caribou hunting grounds.

In 2002-03, after a decade-long wait, 150 families from Davis Inlet were moved to the new location called Natuashish. For the first time — 35 years after they were originally promised — the Innu enjoyed homes with running water and electricity. Unfortunately, many of the old problems followed the Innu to Natuashish. Alcohol abuse continued to plague the town and family violence emerged as a pressing concern. A Healing Strategy is being funded federally, a holistic program aimed at combating the root problems in the community and providing support for effective long-term solutions.

Present Day Innu

The Innu continue to work to strengthen their culture. Central to their efforts are semi-annual camp gatherings. Here, elders participate in private and public mokushans, where they consume sacred caribou fat and bone marrow in homage to the important animal. The also discuss issues such as health and education that affect their community.

Today, most Innu live in one of two Labrador communities — Sheshatshui on Lake Melville and Natuashish on the northern coast. They consider themselves part of the Innu Nation, which included the Innu people of Quebec. It is estimated there about 2,500 Innu in the province.

MI'KMAQ

In 2011, the Qalipu Mi'kmaq First Nation Band was created with Brendan Sheppard as its chief. Its establishment was the culmination of a long process that formally began in 1989. At that time, the Federation of Newfoundland Indians representing nine Mi'kmaq communities, teamed with chiefs from six affiliated groups and initiated a Federal Court Action for the Mi'kmaq to gain eligibility under the Indian Act.

The Qalipu Mi'kmaq are now recognized as a band without reserve land, and members are entitled to benefits and services under the Indian Act. All of Mi'kmaq territory is known as Mi'kma'ki and the Newfoundland and Labrador part of the territory is called Ktaqamkuk.

The Mi'kmaq of Newfoundland and Labrador have a story explaining the creation of the Island of Newfoundland. When the Great Spirit, Manitou, was creating the North American continent, he had extra material — rocks, swamps and trees. He threw this aside, tossing it into the sea to the northeast. Manitou called this pile of rocks, swamps and trees Wee-soc-kadao — and so the Island of Newfoundland came to be.

Mi'kmaq oral tradition holds that they have lived on the Island of Newfoundland permanently since before the arrival of Europeans. Others contend that although the Mi'kmaq occasionally journeyed to Newfoundland to fish and hunt, they did not live there permanently until the late 1760s, when their harsh treatment at the hands of the

British in Nova Scotia led many of them to relocate to Newfoundland, a region under lighter British control.

The last spike of the trans-Newfoundland railway signaled progress to many in the Colony, but for the Mi'kmaq it heralded the end of a traditional way of life. When the railroad was completed in 1898, it opened up the interior to white hunters. After 1905, loggers hunting caribou in the massive area given to the pulpwood mill in Grand Falls, also contributed to the animal's population decline, and by 1930 this mainstay of the Mi'kmaq diet had been hunted to near extinction.

Today, there is one federally recognized Mi'kmaq reserve in Newfoundland and Labrador and it is known as Miawpukwek, or Conne River First Nation. It is estimated there are 2,947 Mi'kmaq Miawepukwek and 23,934 Mi'kmaq Qalipu in the province.

THE VIKINGS ARRIVE 500 YEARS BEFORE COLUMBUS

While it is known that aboriginal peoples inhabited what today is Newfoundland and Labrador for more than 8,000 year, before the first Europeans arrived, the discovery that Vikings arrived in the region came as somewhat of a surprise to many historians and academics.

For centuries, however, Norse sagas offered clues that Vikings had visited North America long before Columbus "discovered" the continent in 1492. In the 1960s, Helga and Anne Stine Ingstad's archaeological findings at L'Anse aux Meadows on the northernmost tip on the Northern Peninsula showed that the Norse encountered the province's First People five centuries before European fishermen dropped anchor off the coast.

The archaeological findings offered evidence of an ancient Norse settlement dating to about 1000 AD, the year Leif Eriksson came ashore somewhere along North America's east coast. Debate surrounds the precise location of this landing, but the L'Anse aux Meadows discovery confirms Viking settlement and some believe that Newfoundland may have been the site of the Viking's "Vinland."

Based on the idea that the Old Norse name "Vinland," mentioned in the Icelandic Sagas, meant "wine-land," historians had long speculated that the region contained wild grapes. Because of this, the common hypothesis prior to the Ingstads' theories was that the Vinland region existed somewhere south of the Northern Massachusetts coast, because that is roughly as far north as grapes grow naturally.

The Ingstads doubted this theory, saying, "that the name Vinland probably means land of meadows ... and includes a peninsula." This speculation was based on the belief that the Norse would not have been comfortable settling in areas along the American Atlantic coast.

Ancient homes of Viking settlers in L'Anse aux Meadows National Historic Site.

ARCHAEOLOGICAL FINDINGS

In 1960, George Decker, a citizen of the small fishing hamlet of L'Anse aux Meadows, led Helge Ingstad to a group of mounds near the village that the locals called the "old Indian camp." These grass-covered bumps looked like the remains of houses.

Helge Ingstad and Anne Stine Ingstad carried out seven archaeological excavations there from 1961 to 1968. They investigated eight complete house sites, as well as the remains of a ninth. They determined that the site was of Norse origin because of definitive similarities between the characteristics of structures and artifacts found at the site, compared to sites in Greenland and Iceland from around 1000 CE.

How the village itself came to be named L'Anse aux Meadows is not clear. Parks Canada, which manages the site, states that the current name was Anglicized from "Anse à la Médée" after English speakers settled in the area. Another possibility is that "L'Anse aux Meadows" is a corruption of the French designation "L'Anse aux Méduses," which means "Jellyfish Cove." The shift from "Méduses" to "Meadows" may have occurred because the landscape in the area tends to be open, with meadows.

It is known that a second group of Viking settlers, with as many as 135 men and 15 women spent several summers at L'Anse aux Meadows gathering wood and pelts that were in much demand in Greenland. On these visits the Vikings met, and for a time, traded with local people. Known to the Vikings as Skraelings, they were most likely Beothuk or Innu.

For unknown reasons, however, relations soured. Outnumbered by the unwelcoming Skraelings, the Vikings returned to Greenland, having spent fewer than five years in North America.

Archeologists are still piecing together fragments of these long-ago stories, and the many historical sites found throughout this place have unique and meaningful tales to tell, but today L'Anse aux Meadows is the most famous site of a Norse or Viking settlement in North America. It was named a UNESCO World Heritage Site in 1978.

Although a possible Norse settlement has been found in southern Newfoundland at Point Rosee, L'Anse aux Meadows is currently the only confirmed Norse site in North America outside of Greenland. It represents the farthest-known extent of European exploration and settlement of the New World, before the voyages of Christopher Columbus almost 500 years later.

A night scene of the statue of John Cabot in Bristol, England. Cabot is recognized as the discoverer of Newfoundland.

JOHN CABOT DISCOVERS NEWFOUNDLAND

Canadian children are taught that John Cabot was an Italian navigator and explorer whose 1497 discovery of parts of North America, under the commission of Henry VII of England, is commonly held to have been the first European exploration of the mainland of North America, since the Norse Vikings' visits to Vinland in the 11th Century.

The Canadian and British governments have both accepted a widely held conclusion that the landing site was at Cape Bonavista, Newfoundland, on June 24, 1497.

Italian sailor and explorer John Cabot was born Giovanni Caboto around 1450. In 1497, Cabot traveled by sea to Canada, where he made a claim to the land for England, mistaking the North American land for Asia.

According to the article "John Cabot Biography" on the The Biography.com website,

Cabot was the son of a spice merchant, Giulio Caboto, in Genoa. At age 11, his family moved to Venice, where he learned sailing and navigation from Italian seamen and merchants.

In 1474, John Cabot married a girl named Mattea and eventually became the father of three sons — Ludovico, Sancto and Sebastiano. Sebastiano would later follow in his father's footsteps, becoming an explorer in his own right. In 1476, Cabot officially became a Venetian citizen and began conducting trade in the eastern Mediterranean. Records indicate that he got into financial trouble and left Venice as a debtor in November 1488.

During this time, Cabot became inspired by the discoveries of Bartolomeu Dias and Christopher Columbus. Like Columbus, Cabot believed that sailing west from Europe was the shorter route to Asia. Hearing of opportunities in England, Cabot traveled there and met with King Henry VII, who gave him a grant to "seeke out, discover, and finde" new lands for England.

Setting Sail

In early May of 1497, Cabot left Bristol, England, on the *Matthew*, a fast and able ship weighing 50 tons, with a crew of 18 men. Cabot and his crew sailed west and north under Cabot's belief that the route to Asia would be shorter from northern Europe than Columbus's voyage along the trade winds.

On June 24, 1497, 50 days into the voyage, Cabot landed on the east coast of North America, though the precise location of this landing is subject to controversy. Some historians believe that Cabot landed at Cape Breton Island or mainland Nova Scotia. Others believe he may have landed at Newfoundland, Labrador or even Maine.

Though the *Matthew*'s logs are incomplete, it is believed that John Cabot went ashore with a small party and claimed the land for the King of England. The ship sailed for England in July 1497 and arrived in Bristol on August 6, 1497.

Cabot was soon rewarded with a pension of £20 and the gratitude of King Henry VII. In February 1498, he was given permission to make a new voyage to North America.

In May 1498, John Cabot departed from Bristol with five ships and a crew of 300 men. The ships carried ample provisions and small samplings of cloth, lace points and other "trifles," suggesting an expectation of fostering trade with indigenous people. En route, one ship became disabled and sailed to Ireland, while the other four ships continued on.

From this point, there is only speculation as to the fate of the voyage and John Cabot. For many years, it was believed that the ships were lost at sea. More recently, however, documents have emerged that place Cabot in England in 1500, laying speculation that he and his crew actually survived the voyage.

Historians have also found evidence to suggest that Cabot's expedition explored the eastern Canadian coast, and that a priest accompanying the expedition might have established a Christian settlement in Newfoundland. What can be said with some certainty is that John Cabot claimed North America for England, setting the course for England's rise to power in the 16th and 17th centuries.

AN HISTORIC SITE

With a population of roughly 800 people, the town of Cupids on Conception Bay is the oldest continuously settled official British colony in Canada.

It was established in 1610, when Englishman John Guy and his backers brought a boatload of settlers and set up a plantation in what was then known as Cuper's Cove. It was the second English colony in North America after Jamestown, Virginia, founded in 1607.

According to a tourism website for Newfoundland and Labrador, the people of Cuper's Cove cleared the land and constructed dwellings, fortifications and boats. They fished, farmed, explored for minerals, and tried to establish fur trading with the Beothuk, the now extinct aboriginal people.

The colony was plagued by pirate attacks including the Pirate Admiral Peter Easton, as well as the harsh conditions of early settlement.

The first recorded birth of an English child in Canada took place at Cupids.

The famous Native American Squanto lived in Cupids from 1616–1618. He was captured by the English, travelled to Europe before returning to North America, and ended up greeting the Pilgrim Fathers — in English — at Plymouth Rock.

Around the year 1700, settlers abandoned the original plantation site in favour of a secondary settlement, but the secret of its exact location was lost for more than 250 years. Today, though, archaeologists are uncovering the secrets of that second location piece by piece.

A provincial historic site, Cupids has also been known as Coopers, Coper's Cove, Cuper's Cove and Cuperts.

FIRST ENGLISH BURIAL GROUNDS

A gravesite discovered in Newfoundland is believed to be the oldest English cemetery in Canada. It is a 400-year-old burial ground used by the original settlers at the historic Conception Bay village of Cupids.

The cemetery plot was exposed as part of an ongoing excavation of the 17th-century settlement that marked the beginning of a permanent British presence in the future Canada.

The gravesites located close to the remnants of structures from the original 1610 colony, suggest they hold some of the oldest European remains in Canada.

The earliest Newfoundland graves would have been dug a few years after French colonists at St. Croix Island — an ill-fated settlement site near the mouth of the St. Croix River between Maine and New Brunswick — were forced to bury about 35 members of their party who died of scurvy during their harrowing first winter of 1604-05.

In 2003, U.S. and Canadian archeologists, excavating graves at that site, found the earliest known evidence of an autopsy in the New World, a skull sawed open by Champlain's barber-surgeon in an apparent attempt to understand the disease that was killing the colonists.

THE GOLDEN AGE OF PIRATES

Piracy was a phenomenon that was not limited to the Caribbean region. In fact, during what has been called the Golden Age of Pirates, the marauders not only roamed off the coast of Africa and the Caribbean, but also carried out their trade along the North American coastline.

Piracy, seizure and robbery of craft at sea, has played a major role in Maritime history and folklore for centuries. For instance, one of the greatest legends of all time suggests that the treasure of William Kidd, who was hanged in 1701, is reputed to be buried on Nova Scotia's fabled Oak Island.

Newfoundland's pirate legacy

Peter Easton

One of the most notorious pirates to ply the waters around Newfoundland and Labrador was Peter Easton.

Even before John Guy established Newfoundland's first settlement at Cupid's in 1610, the notorious "Pirate Admiral" as he was known, was plying the waters with as many as 40 ships and 5,000 pirate sailors.

Easton was sent to Newfoundland in 1602, a loyal privateer serving Queen Elizabeth in charge of protecting the fishing fleet. During these times, fishing vessels would carry arms and small cannons to protect the valuable cargo of fish from pirates and foreign vessels. Under Easton's commission, he could legally press-gang local fishermen into service for him. He could also attack the ships and wharves of the enemy as much as he wished, especially the much hated Spanish.

With the accession of King James I to the throne and the more peaceful relations that followed, privateers' letter of commission were cancelled and some of them, including Easton, turned to piracy to make a living.

Easton knew the Atlantic intimately and he practiced his new "profession" with zeal, from the Caribbean to Newfoundland and the Azores. In Newfoundland, he plundered habours and ships, confiscating treasure and pressing sailors into his service. He once captured 30 ships in St. John's Harbour in one raid, taking men and money. He was rumoured to have captured great fortunes from the Spanish in the Caribbean.

By 1611, his international operations were based in Harbour Grace, Newfoundland, and he later moved them to Ferryland. By that point in time, Easton was in charge of ten pirate ships. He raided and plundered both English and foreign vessels and the harbours of Newfoundland, press-ganging fishermen into his service along the way.

In 1614, Easton sought a pardon for his pirating ways, which James I, pleased with Easton's harassment of the French, offered him. News of it was slow to reach the pirate, however, and he set off on another southern escapade in the meantime to enhance his fortune and avoid capture.

Eventually, Easton retired to Villefranche, Savoy, a free port for pirates in the south of France where he became part of the elite, married a wealthy woman and acquired the title "Marquis of Savoy." He was never overtaken or captured by any fleet commissioned to hunt him down. It is believed Easton died around the year 1620.

Bartholomew Roberts

The history of Newfoundland is rich with tales and lore of pirates pillaging and plundering along its rugged coastline.

Another notorious pirate was Bartholomew Roberts. Born in Pembrokeshire, Wales, sometime before 1682, Roberts was known as "The Puritan Pirate" because he forbade excessive immoral conduct on board his ships.

Having appeared off the coast of Nova Scotia in June 1720, he made for Trepassey, Newfoundland where, in a pre-dawn raid with a single ship, he captured 22 merchant ships and four vessels, and sank a few fishing boats. Proceeding to the Grand Banks, he then captured six French vessels.

Roberts, who during his four-year career captured 400 ships, was apprehended in 1722 by ships of the Royal Navy off West Africa. After he quit Canadian waters he made for the African coast. He was killed in February 1772 when he engaged a British ship off Cape Lopez. Most of his surviving crewmen were executed or sentenced to slavery.

When Roberts died, his death marked the end of the "Golden Age of Piracy."

In addition to Easton and Roberts, several other pirates of note roamed the coastline of Newfoundland several centuries ago.

For starters, there was Henry Mainwaring, the master mariner who was actually sent to Newfoundland to arrest Peter Easton. Upon arriving in Newfoundland, however, he fell in love with pirating and took up the business himself, assuming Easton's place when he retired.

Another well-known pirate was John Nutt. He patrolled the waters off Newfoundland from 1620 to 1623 and had the distinction of being on the Crown's blacklist. After his relatively short career, he requested and received a pardon. When he returned home, he was nonetheless imprisoned and sentenced to hang. Friends in high places managed to secure him a last minute pardon.

Marquis de la Rade, the French pirate and his 400 men, wrought havoc on the shores of Newfoundland in the early 17th Century. In 1628, he and his men attacked and pillaged English settlers at Trinity and Conception Bay.

The notorious Edward Low was one of the most brutal pirates to ply the North Atlantic waters. Even his pirate friends were shocked by Low's brutality. He was especially fond of torturing victims, forcing them to eat their own amputated lips or ears. His cruelty was visited upon the whole of the Atlantic, and Newfoundland did not escape. He was eventually executed for his crimes.

Old view of St. John's (Prince of Wales arrival). Created by Lebreton after photo of Miot, published on L'Illustration, Journal Universel, Paris, 1860.

THE OLDEST ON THE CONTINENT

St. John's, the capital and largest city in Newfoundland and Labrador, has the distinction of being the oldest city in North America.

Officially incorporated as a city in 1888 and known as the City of Legends, St. John's is located on the eastern tip of the Avalon Peninsula. With a population of 214,285 as of July 1, 2015, it is the second largest city in Atlantic Canada after Halifax and the 20th largest in Canada.

Its name has been attributed to the feast day of John The Baptist, when John Cabot was believed to have sailed into the harbour in 1497, and also to a Basque fishing town with the same name.

Ancient homes of Viking settlers in L'Anse aux Meadows National Historic Site.

Following is a list of the oldest buildings in the province:

1. **Anderson House, St. John's, 1805**

    Of the many historical structures in St. John's, Anderson House, located at 42 Powers Court, is believed to be the oldest structure in the city. Originally built for James Anderson, who was a Sergeant in the militia, the house is of modest construction and is an excellent example of 19th Century homes built circa 1804. It was built on land that was purchased from Dr. Jonathan Ogden, a Newfoundland chief justice, in 1802. The house has found use as both a military and private residence. It was used as a military barracks with a (now demolished) section of the house used to stable horses. It has been home to a number of families and on March 23, 1996, the Anderson House became a Registered Heritage Structure by the Heritage Foundation of Newfoundland and Labrador.

2. **Alexander House, Bonavista, 1811-14**
   William Alexander House is a two and a half storey, wooden framed building, designed in the Georgian style by Alexander Strathie. It is designated as a Registered Heritage Structure due to its historical, architectural and environmental values and is historically valuable for its age and its association with William Alexander. William Alexander House was built between 1811 and 1814 and is the oldest residential structure in Newfoundland that has been assigned a date.

3. **Government House, St. John's, 1831**
   Completed in 1831, the building was designed by Governor Sire Thomas Cochrane. Government House is constructed of red sandstone quarried from Signal Hill by labourers from Scotland, and it was built with a "dry moat" surrounding it. Government House is the residence of the Lt. Governor of Newfoundland and Labrador.

4. **Hebron Moravian Mission, Hebron, 1830s**
   The surviving elements of Hebron Mission consist of a long interconnected series of buildings, including a church, mission house, and finally a store. The design has a Germanic flavor, characterized by the steep, elongated roof punctuated by small dormer windows. The cupola is typical of church architecture of south-eastern Europe, from whence came the Moravians. Other buildings, including a forge, carpenter's shop, and other support structures remain. Hebron Mission was declared a national historic site in 1976 because it provided religious instruction to the local Inuit and was also an educational, commercial and medical centre. It is one of only a representative examples in North America of Moravian mission architecture.

5. **Cathedral of St. John the Baptist, St. John's, 1847**
   A National Historic Site, this Gothic Revival structure was designed by the famous church architect Sir George Gilbert Scott in 1847 and was first completed in 1885. After being destroyed in the Great Fire of 1892, it was rebuilt inside the original stonewalls following Scott's design. The bulk of the walls are composed of Newfoundland Bluestone from the Southside Hills. The building as it stands is incomplete. Parts of the ceiling remain to be finished and the central tower in Scott's original design has never been built.

6. **Bank of British North America Building, St. John's, 1849**
   Located at 276 Duckworth Street, it is now known as the Anna Templeton Center. Erected in 1849 as a three-storey structure, it had a fourth storey added in 1885. After the Great Fire of 1892, the bank was reconstructed inside its partially gutted shell. The building was used as a bank from 1849 to the 1980's and the upper storey served for a time as a residence for the bank manager. The stained glass windows in the east side have panels with the letters "CB" for the Commercial Bank that occupied the building from 1858 to 1895.

7. **Colonial Building, St. John's, 1850**
   Built in 1850, the white limestone building housed the Newfoundland legislature until 1959. This building was the scene of many historic events, including Newfoundland's first bank robbery (there was a savings bank in the basement), the 1887 Jubilee Ball in honour of Queen Victoria, and several violent riots, the most recent of which was in 1932 when an angry mob tried to lynch Prime Minister Sir Richard Squires. It currently houses the Provincial Archives.

8. **Church of St. James the Apostle, Battle Harbour, 1852**
   Construction began on St. James the Apostle Anglican Church in 1852. When it finished in 1857, the church became the focal point for the spiritual needs of both the resident and migratory population. This is the oldest, non-Moravaian church in Labrador. The building is typical of Anglican mission churches built throughout Newfoundland in the nineteenth Century. The furnishings, as far as can be determined, date from its consecration, and reflect the Gothic theme of the church.

9. **Basilica of St. John The Baptist, St. John's, 1855**
   With its twin 43-metre-high towers and location on the high hill on the northern side of the harbour, the Basilica has long been the dominant feature of the St. John's skyline. Begun in 1841 and completed in 1850, the Military Road structure was consecrated as a cathedral in 1855. At that time, it was the largest church in North America. Built in the shape of a Latin cross, it was declared a minor Basilica on its centenary in 1955. It is now a national historic site.

10. **Point Amour Lighthouse, Point Amour, 1854-57**

Located on Point Amour in southern Labrador, it was completed in 1857. It is the tallest lighthouse in Atlantic Canada and the second tallest in Canada, reaching a height of 109 feet (33 m). The cylindrical tower is built of limestone and is painted white with a black band. It was built in the series of Imperial Towers and is designated a provincial historic site.

Point Amour lighthouse on the coast of Labrador.

In addition to these historically important structures, other notable buildings in the city of St. John's include:

Saint Bonaventure's College, St. John's

St. Bonaventure's College (commonly called St. Bon's) is an independent kindergarten to grade 12 Catholic School. It is located in the historic centre of St. John's adjacent to the Roman Catholic Basilica of St. John the Baptist. The school was founded by the Franciscans in 1857, and from 1889, was administered by the Irish Christian Brothers. In 1999, St. Bon's became an independent Roman Catholic School in the Jesuit Tradition. In 2003, St. Bon's became a member of the Jesuit Secondary School Association.

Market House Hill

The steps going up the side of the courthouse are situated on an area once known as Market House Hill. In the 19th Century, this was an important gathering place for the people of St. John's. In addition to being the grounds of the city's court, post office, and produce market, it was a center for open-air auctions and the site of the public gallows. The last public hanging in Newfoundland took place on this hill in January of 1835 when a man named John Flood was executed for highway robbery.

Signal Hill

Originally known as the Lookout it became Signal Hill in 1762 whereby merchants, customs officials, and the harbour pilot could prepare docking facilities for incoming vessels after receiving flag signals from atop the hill.

Cabot Tower

Built by Samuel Garrison between 1898 and 1900, and constructed of local granite, Cabot Tower was built to commemorate Newfoundland's discovery by John Cabot and Queen Victoria's Diamond Jubilee. Marconi received the first wireless message on December 21, 1901 near Cabot Tower.

Yellow Belly Corner Buildings

This area was given its name after the colour of sashes worn by one of the various Irish factions who would meet and fight on this site in the early 19th Century. The buildings were constructed after the fire of 1846 and are an excellent example of the buildings found in the downtown prior to the Great Fire of 1892. These buildings once served as both commercial and residential premises.

The Crow's Nest

First built as a warehouse after the Great Fire of 1892, the building then known as "The Old Butler Building" is now best known as the place that houses one of St. John's most exclusive clubs, the Crow's Nest. It was built on the same ground where an old inn called "The Ship" was located two centuries earlier.

During the building's first 50 years it was primarily a warehouse. That changed in 1942. With the Second World War raging in Europe, many naval vessels made St. John's a port of call. Captain E.R. Mainguy was the officer in charge of navy escort ships stationed in St. John's. With the assistance of Lady Dorothy Outerbridge, he was able to obtain space for a club where officers could visit when not on duty.

Lady Outerbridge was able to find space on the fourth floor of the warehouse and obtained it for the rent of $1 per year.

Considered a significant structure by the Canadian Navy, the Crow's Nest and surrounding buildings were recognized as a Registered Heritage Structure in April 1990 by the Heritage Foundation of Newfoundland and Labrador.

Majestic Theatre

One of the many theatres once located in the downtown, this building at one point hosted a large unruly crowd in 1932 that gathered prior to marching to the Colonial Building and attempted to lynch the Prime Minister. It now serves as a local bar and one of the many downtown watering holes.

George Street United Church

This is the oldest surviving Methodist church in St. John's. The church is built of Newfoundland stone and slate quarried from Southside Hills.

Gower Street United Church

This visibly striking church, sometimes called the "Methodist Cathedral", is built of red brick, and was completed in 1896 after the previous church on the site was destroyed in the Great Fire of 1892. The first of the three churches that have occupied the site was started in 1816. The present church once had a spire, but deterioration caused it to be removed several years ago.

St. Andrew's Church

On Harvey Road, stands an imposing building with an impressive spire. St. Andrew's was built in 1894 after the original Presbyterian Church on Duckworth Street was destroyed in the Great Fire of 1892. The "Kirk", as it is also known, is an excellent example of the Gothic Revival style.

St. Thomas' Garrison Church

A striking black wooden building opened in 1836, St. Thomas Anglican Church is the oldest church in St. John's. Located at the corner of Military and King's Bridge Roads, it originally served the members of the British Garrison at Fort William, which stood at the nearby site now occupied by the Hotel Newfoundland. Though made of wood, the church survived the Great Fires of 1846 and 1892 because it was located outside the main areas of destruction. The Great Gale of 1846 moved St. Thomas' six inches on its foundation and wings were consequently added to the building to stabilize it.

Visible in the St. John's skyline are the Basilica of St. John's the Baptist, The Rooms, St. Andrew's Church, and St. John's the Baptist Anglican Cathedral.

REACH FOR THE SKY

Following are the 10 tallest buildings in St. John's,

1. Confederation Building completed in 1959, 64 m (210 ft)
2. John Cabot Place completed in 1996, 63 m (207 ft)
3. St. Patrick's Church completed in 1888, 60 m (197 ft)
4. Cabot Place completed in 1988, 53 m (174 ft)
5. Delta St. John's Hotel completed in 1987, 51 m (167 ft)
6. Scotia Centre completed in 1987, 50 m (164 ft)
7. Southcott Hall completed in 1964, 49 m (161 ft)
8. Fortis Building completed in 1969, 49 m (161 ft)
9. TD Place completed in 1981, 45 m (148 ft)
10. Atlantic Place completed in 1975, 43 m (141 ft)

Cape Bonavista Lighthouse built in 1842 is now a provincial historic site.

LET THERE BE LIGHT

As the official government website points out, with over 29,000 km of twisting coastline, laden with submerged rocks, inlets, icebergs and fog, it's no wonder Newfoundland and Labrador has several hundred navigational lights clinging to its shores. Long before electricity, motorboats and coast guards, fishermen and sailors relied on lighthouses and their keepers to guide them safe from peril.

This rugged place has known its fair share of shipwrecks, tragedies that occurred before lighthouses were constructed. Hundreds of stories of rescues have been passed down through for centuries.

Newfoundland and Labrador established its first permanent lighthouse in 1813 at Fort Amherst, the entrance to St. John's Harbour. Since then, hundreds of lighthouses and small beacons took up residence along the shores, usually painted in different styles — such as plain white or candy-striped — to help sailors recognize the location they were approaching.

The provincial website says Cape Race Lighthouse was the location for Newfoundland's first wireless communication station and was established a couple of years after the first transatlantic message was sent by Marconi from Signal Hill. The lighthouse became a centre for reporting news around the world and received the Titanic's distress signal after the vessel hit an iceberg off Newfoundland waters.

NOTABLE LIGHTHOUSES

Cape Spear Lighthouse, a national historic site, is the most easterly point in North America. The lighthouse building is the oldest original lighthouse structure in the province.

Cape Bonavista Lighthouse, just outside the town of Bonavista, is famous as the place where John Cabot first made landfall in Newfoundland in 1497. This is one of the most visited provincial historic sites in the province.

Point Amour Lighthouse, near L'Anse Amour, Labrador, is a provincial historic site and is the second tallest lighthouse in Canada. It was built in 1858 to aid the passage of ships between this country and Europe.

Rose Blanche Lighthouse. The southwest coast of Newfoundland is littered with shipwrecks dating from the early days of European exploration of North America. Most notably, in 1828, in the nearby community of Isle aux Morts, an Irish immigrant ship ran aground and broke apart during a raging storm. For three full days, a 17-year-old girl named Ann Harvey, along with her Newfoundland dog Hairyman, saved passengers and crew by bravely ferrying them to land through fog and lashing wind in a 12-foot skiff. A string of lighthouses was constructed in the area in the 1870s, including the stone lighthouse at Rose Blanche built between 1871 and 1873.

Following is a list of lighthouses in the province of Newfoundland and Labrador,

    Bacalhao Island Light

    Baccalieu Island Light

    Bay Bulls Light

    Bear Cove Point Light

    Bell Island Light

    Belle Island South End Lights

    Belle Isle Northeast Light

    Belleoram Light

    Boar Island Light

    Brigus Light

    Broad Cove Point Range Lights

Brunette Island Light
Burnt Point Light
Cabot Islands Light
Camp Islands Light
Cape Anguille Light
Cape Bauld Light
Cape Bonavista Light
Cape Norman Light
Cape Pine Light
Cape Race Light
Cape Ray Light
Cape Spear Light
Cape St. Francis Light
Cape St. Mary's Light
Change Islands Light
Channel Head Light
Colombier Islands Light
Conche Light
Cow Head Light
Dawson Point Light
Double Island Light
English Harbour West Light
Ferryland Head Light
Flowers Island Light
Fort Amherst Light
Fort Point Light (Newfoundland)
Fortune Head Light
Fox Point Light
François Bay Light
Frenchman's Head Light
Garnish Light
Grand Bank Light
Green Island Light (Catalina)
Green Island Light (Fortune Bay)

Green Point Light
Gull Island Light
Hants Harbour Light
Harbour Point Light
Heart's Content Light
Ireland Island Light
Keppel Island Light
Kings Cove Head Light
La Haye Point Light
Little Burin Island Light
Little Denier Island Light
Lobster Cove Head Light
Long Island East End Light
Long Island Light (Newfoundland)
Long Point Lighthouse
Manuel Island Light (Labrador)
Manuel Island Light (Newfoundland)
Marticot Island Light
Middle Head Light
New Férolle Peninsula Light
North Penguin Island Light
Northwest Head Light
Offer Wadham Island Light
Pack's Harbour Light
Peckford Island Light
Point Amour Lighthouse
Point Latine Light
Point Verde Light
Pointe Riche Light
Powles Head Light
Puffin Island Light
Random Head Harbour Light
Red Island Light
Rocky Point Light

Rose Blanche Light
Saddle Island Light
Salmon Point Light
Sandy Point Island Light
Sloop Harbour Point Light
South Head Light
St. Jacques Island Light
St. Lawrence Point Light
St. Modeste Island Light
Surgeon Cove Point Light
Tides Cove Point Light
Twillingate Light
Westport Cove Light
White Point Light
Winsor Harbour Island Light
Woody Point Light

UNESCO SITES

The United Nations Educational, Scientific, and Cultural Organization (UNESCO) has identified just over 800 places in the world that are of outstanding natural and cultural significance.

There are 17 in Canada, and three are in Newfoundland and Labrador. Two of them — Gros Morne National Park and L'Anse aux Meadows National Historic Site — are located on the west coast of the Island of Newfoundland. The third — Red Bay National Historic Site — is part of the Labrador Coastal Drive. It can be reached via ferry from St. Barbe, Newfoundland, to Blanc Sablon, Quebec.

Below, Parks Canada describes each of the sites:

Inland fjord between large steep cliffs with some green vegetation on rock face, at Western Brook Pond, Gros Morne National Park.

Gros Morne National Park — Soaring fjords and moody mountains tower above a diverse panorama of beaches and bogs, forests and barren cliffs. Shaped by colliding continents and grinding glaciers, Gros Morne's ancient landscape is a UNESCO World Heritage Site. Wander coastal pathways and beachcomb among sea stacks. Cruise the dramatic, sheer-walled gorge of Western Brook Pond. Spot moose and caribou. Hike to alpine highlands where Arctic hare and ptarmigan thrive on tundra, and explore the colourful culture of nearby seaside villages.

L'Anse aux Meadows National Historic Site — At the tip of Newfoundland's Great Northern Peninsula, lies the first known evidence of European presence in the Americas.

Here, a Norse expedition sailed from Greenland, building a small encampment of timber-and-sod buildings over 1000 years ago. Against a stunning backdrop of rugged cliffs, bog, and coastline, discover the fascinating archaeological remains of the Viking encampment, declared a UNESCO World Heritage Site in 1978.

Red Bay National Historic Site — During the mid-16th Century, large numbers of right and bowhead whales drew whalers from the Basque region of Spain and France to the Strait of Belle Isle, where they established a major whaling port at Red Bay. For some 70 years, Basque whalers made the dangerous, month-long journey across the Atlantic to hunt whales and produce the oil that lit the lamps of Europe.

See original Basque artifacts, remains, and restored chalupa at this national historic site and World Heritage Site.

FIRST WORLD WAR

When Britain entered the First World War on August 4, 1914, Newfoundland — which was then a British dominion — was suddenly at war, too.

At a time when great pride was taken in being part of the British Empire, the people of Newfoundland reacted enthusiastically to the news of war. Almost 1,000 young men signed up to join the newly-created Newfoundland Regiment by late September, 1914.

According to Veterans Affairs Canada, recruits officially enlisted "for the duration of the war, but not exceeding one year" — a prediction that would prove sadly optimistic, as the conflict would drag on for more than four years.

The first recruits began training in a camp on the outskirts of St. John's. It was a modest start — just getting enough tents proved to be difficult, and some ended up being made from the sails of ships in the harbour.

Providing uniforms was also a challenge. A local shortage of khaki meant they had to use blue fabric for their puttees (wrappings for the lower legs of their uniforms), giving rise to the nickname "the blue puttees" for soldiers of the Newfoundland Regiment.

The regiment's first contingent set sail for Britain on October 3, 1914 and more soldiers soon followed. The Newfoundlanders would train in England and Scotland for months before finally seeing action on an unexpected front — the eastern Mediterranean.

The Allied countries of Britain, France and Russia had declared war on Germany, but were also fighting Germany's other Central Powers partners — Austria-Hungary and the Ottoman Empire. The Ottoman Empire occupied what is now present-day Turkey, the eastern coast of the Mediterranean and parts the Middle East.

The Dardanelles Strait hardship

The Ottoman Empire's control of the Dardanelles Strait, that joined the Mediterranean Sea to the Black Sea, meant it could cut off access to southern Russian seaports. This was important because the Allies wanted to provide Russia with war materials to help the country in its fighting along Europe's Eastern Front, but land transport routes were blocked and other sea routes were difficult.

The Allies decided to create a new front in Turkey to open this supply line to Russia, draw surrounding countries into the war on the Allied side, and help break the stalemate of trench fighting in Europe by pulling enemy resources from other fronts. After preliminary naval engagements, the first Allied troops landed in Turkey's Gallipoli peninsula on April 25, 1915 when the Australian and New Zealand Army Corps (ANZAC) and British forces came ashore. It would be the start of months of trench fighting that soon made it clear an Allied victory there would be much harder than thought.

After almost a year of training, the Newfoundland Regiment learned it would be part of the 29th Division of the British Army fighting in Gallipoli. After a short stay in Egypt, 1,076 Newfoundlanders came ashore along the shores of the Dardanelles Strait on September 20, 1915. The flashes and the sounds of distant artillery and rifle fire quickly told them they were finally in a war zone. The next day, they were shelled by Turkish artillery as they huddled in their shallow dugouts for protection — their welcome to Gallipoli.

The young Newfoundlanders had arrived hoping for action and excitement, but they were soon disappointed. They spent the first months digging trenches, keeping long night watches, spending time on the front line, and learning trench warfare techniques from the ANZAC and British forces that had been fighting there for months.

Conditions were bad. Enemy fire and life in the trenches made the situation miserable for the Newfoundlanders. Even getting enough to drink was difficult. Sometimes, soldiers had to get by on less than a cup of water a day. The weather was harsh and unpredictable. The heat brought swarms of flies that helped spread diseases like dysentery, which hit the Newfoundlanders hard. It could also be surprisingly cold as it was the worst winter in the region in four decades.

Weeks of heavy rains and wind battered the soldiers, turning trenches into flooded ditches. When the rains finally stopped, the weather turned very cold and caused many cases of frostbite. Despite the difficult conditions, the Newfoundlanders persevered and earned their first battle honour when they captured Caribou Hill (a high point used by Turkish snipers) in November, with three men earning medals for their bravery in the fighting.

The lack of a military breakthrough convinced the Allies it was time to withdraw from Gallipoli. It was decided the Newfoundland Regiment would help in the difficult task of covering the evacuation of Allied troops onto waiting ships. This rearguard operation went well and the Newfoundlanders were among the last Allied soldiers to leave Turkey in January 1916.

During the almost four months the Newfoundland Regiment fought at Gallipoli, approximately 30 men died in action and 10 more died of disease. The hardships and death they experienced were a taste of the even harsher experiences that were waiting when they were shifted to Europe's Western Front in April 1916.

Losses

By war's end, more than 6,200 Newfoundland men had served in the regiment. The price was high, however — more than 1,300 died and many returned home with injuries to body and mind that lasted a lifetime. The loss of so many of its finest young citizens, and the toll taken on the survivors was a heavy burden that Newfoundland had to bear for decades.

Gallipoli was the first of many battles that would earn the Newfoundland Regiment an impressive reputation during the First World War. It would go on to fight with distinction in Belgium and France throughout the rest of the conflict. The regiment even earned the title "Royal" in 1917 in recognition of its exceptional service and sacrifice — the only regiment to be honoured this way by the British during the war.

The sacrifices and achievements of the Royal Newfoundland Regiment are not forgotten. July 1 is still marked as Memorial Day in Newfoundland and Labrador in commemoration of the great sacrifices made by the regiment during the First World War.

Information for this item was garnered from the Canada Remembers Program of Veterans Affairs Canada, which encourages all Canadians to learn about the sacrifices and achievements made by those who have served — and continue to serve — during times of war and peace.

WWII

During the Second World War, Canadian and American authorities feared attacks on North American targets and, in fact, German submarines did disembark many agents on the east coasts of both Canada and the United States.

However, Bell Island, located off Newfoundland's Avalon Peninsula in Conception Bay, was among the few places in North America to see, firsthand, the ramifications of wartime combat during the Second World War when, in 1942, German U-boats torpedoed a pier loaded with iron ore, taking out four other vessels in the process.

Upwards of 8,000 tons of ore had been stored at the pier and was awaiting shipping to other locales. A total of 69 people died during the attack. Today, there is a Seamen's Memorial located at Lance Cove at the southern end of the Island to commemorate those who lost their lives during the Second World War-era U-boat assaults.

In another remarkable instance, personnel from German U-boat 537 set up a weather station on the coast of Labrador in 1943. According to a Heritage Newfoundland and Labrador website, this is the only documented landing by armed German combatants on Allied soil in North America.

The U-boat crew lay anchor for 28 hours at Martin Bay, near Cape Chidley, while they worked. While a far greater threat to ships at sea, there was cause to fear attacks launched from U-boats on land-based facilities.

Newfoundland and Labrador was in the war zone despite being thousands of miles away from the main battlefields of Europe. According to the heritage website, ships and U-boats alike were sunk off the coast and there was always the threat of a direct enemy attack.

Blackout regulations were instituted soon after the war began, and provisions were actually made to burn the military facilities in St. John's to the ground in the event of an attack. Furthermore, thousands of Allied troops were stationed in Newfoundland and Labrador during the Second World War, both to protect it and bring the fight to the enemy.

Newfoundland and Labrador not only played an important part in North American defence and the Battle of the Atlantic, but also experienced the war first hand.

"The Allied command had good reason to step up their campaign against the dreaded German submarines, and Newfoundland and Labrador figured prominently in their plans from the beginning," the website says.

Battle of the Atlantic

As the Battle of the Atlantic progressed, aircraft became ever more important in the fight against the U-boats. An aircraft could cover a larger area faster than any warship, and could pounce on an unsuspecting submarine with deadly effect. The head of the U-boat arm, Admiral Karl Dönitz, countered this air threat by equipping his U-boats with heavier anti-aircraft weapons, and by urging his crews to fight it out on the surface. All the same, most U-boat captains preferred to dive out of harm's way. The disadvantage was that the U-boat could lose contact with a convoy and take hours to catch up, if at all.

To this end, the Allies stationed aircraft in Newfoundland at Stephenville, Gander, Argentia and at Torbay, just outside St. John's. As RCAF Station Torbay became fully operational early in 1942, its aircraft supplied convoy protection as far east as the Grand Banks, the U-boats' popular hunting ground.

The operation of the Torbay airbase coincided with greater U-boat activity in local Newfoundland waters. On March 3, 1942, for example, U587 fired three torpedoes at St. John's. One hit Fort Amherst and two more hit the cliffs below Cabot Tower, breaking every window in the building.

Two days previous, a Liberator aircraft out of Argentia, flown by Ensign William Tepune, caught U-656, under Kaptänleutnant Ernst Kröning, on the surface in broad daylight a mere 40 kilometres south of Trepassey and destroyed it. This sinking gave rise to one of the most famous radio signals of the war — "Sighted Sub, Sank Same."

FIVE FAST FACTS

1 The highest-scoring Newfoundlander to play in the NHL is Michael Ryder. Born in Bonavista in 1980, Ryder has tallied well over 450 points in an NHL career that has seen him play for Montreal, Boston, Dallas and New Jersey. Ryder played for the Bonavista Saints in the Newfoundland Amateur Hockey Association in 1996-97. He was selected by the Montreal Canadiens in the eighth round of the 1998 NHL draft.

2 Newfoundland was originally slated to become a Canadian province on April 1, 1949. Fearful of becoming the "fools" of Canadian Confederation, the province instead opted to join Canada technically in the dying minutes of March 31. The official swearing in and parties were delayed until April 2.

3 "Tilts" are small seasonal homes along the Labrador coast. They were known for their unique wallpaper. Although many residents could not read, they decorated walls with pages of newspapers and magazines.

4 Between 1857 and 1949, Newfoundland issued about 300 of its own postage stamps. These stamps can still be used in Canada.

5 Early Newfoundland "currency" consisted of dried codfish.

Stamp printed by Newfoundland (circa 1923) shows South West Arm, Trinity.

FIVE FAST FACTS

1 Memorial University of Newfoundland is the largest university in Atlantic Canada.

2 In 1961, legendary entertainer, Bob Hope performed in Labrador at the Goose Bay Air Force Base and in Newfoundland at Argentia and at Harmon AFB in Stephenville, all American military bases. Many other well-known celebrities, including Elvis Presley, Marilyn Munro and Frank Sinatra also performed at bases in the province.

3 Newfoundland's first commercial radio station, VOGY, hit the airwaves on September 12, 1932. It broadcast from a studio in St. John's posh Crosbie Hotel.

4 In 1000 AD, Norse Vikings landed near Black Duck Brook at L'Anse aux Meadow.

5 In 1497, Italian explorer John Cabot, sailing under the English flag, landed on the coast of Newfoundland. Cabot claimed the "new found land" for England.

INVENTIONS

JUST A GAS

The first, widely used military gas mask was introduced by a Newfoundlander in 1915.

A physician named Cluny MacPherson, who was born on March 18, 1879, in St. John's, Newfoundland, is credited for inventing the first gas mask used on the battlefield.

During the First World War, the German army used poison gas for the first time, against Allied troops at Ypres, Belgium in 1915. A soldier's only protection was to breathe through a handkerchief or other small piece of fabric soaked in urine.

Out of necessity, Dr. MacPherson quickly came up with the idea of a gas mask made of fabric and metal. Using a helmet taken from a captured German prisoner, he added a canvas hood with eyepieces and a breathing tube. The helmet was treated with chemicals that would absorb the chlorine used in the gas attacks.

After a few improvements, Dr. MacPherson's helmet became the first gas mask to be used by the British army. At the time, his invention was heralded as the most important protective device of the First World War, protecting countless soldiers from blindness, disfigurement or injury to their throats and lungs.

Dr. MacPherson, who received his medical education from Methodist College and McGill University, started the first St. John Ambulance Brigade in Newfoundland after working with the St. John Ambulance Association. He served as the principal medical officer for the St. John Ambulance Brigade of the first Newfoundland Regiment during the First World War.

After suffering a war injury, Dr. MacPherson returned to Newfoundland to serve as the Director of the military medical service and later served as the President of the St. John's Clinical Society and the Newfoundland Medical Association. He was awarded many honours for his contributions to medical science.

Dr. MacPherson married Eleanora Thompson in 1902. His home at 65 Rennie's Mill Road, where he served as secretary, treasurer and registrar for the Newfoundland Medical Society now has historic designation. He died on November 16, 1966.

FIVE FAST FACTS

1 In 1662, Plaisance (now Placentia), a French capital, was founded with a governor and 80 settlers, when King Louis XIV decided fortification and colonization were needed to protect French fishing grounds.

2 The Treaty of Paris, signed in 1763, ended the Seven Years' War and, with it, French claims to North America. France retained the Islands of St. Pierre and Miquelon and the right to catch and dry fish along Newfoundland's French Shore, providing French fishermen left the colony each season by September 10.

3 The government passed legislation in 1863 to establish the colony's money as dollars and cents. The first one-, five-, ten-, twenty- and two-hundred-cent coins were issued in 1865.

4 The 4,828 km-long Atlantic cable, laid from Ireland by the steamship *The Great Eastern*, is landed at Heart's Content in 1866. It is the first telegraph between Europe and North America.

5 Newfoundland voted "no" to joining the Canadian federation in 1869 because citizens were unsure of whether a union with other British colonies would raise or lower taxes, improve services or debilitate the economy.

LAW AND ORDER

LEGAL NOTES

- In 1791, the British Parliament passed legislation to create the first civil court in the Newfoundland colony. John Reeves was appointed the first judge in Newfoundland and, in 1792, its first Chief Justice.

- In 1824, the British Parliament restricted the powers of Newfoundland's surrogate courts, repealed the authority of fishing admirals, and established a permanent Supreme Court with civil and criminal jurisdictions on and off shore.

SHOOT TO KILL

A duel is a formal armed combat between two people in the presence of witnesses, to settle differences or a point of honour. Duels were recorded in New France (Quebec) as early as 1646. The last known duel in Canada, however, occurred in 1826 at St John's, Newfoundland.

Most incidents ended without injury, but there were some fatal encounters — at least nine died in New France, two in Lower Canada, five in Upper Canada, two each in Nova Scotia and New Brunswick, and one in Newfoundland.

Captain Mark Rudkin, an Irish native and 22-year veteran of the British Army, was stationed at St. John's. He has the distinction of being the last known person to duel in Newfoundland, which led to the death of Ensign John Philpot who was posted with the Royal Veteran Companies, also stationed at St. John's.

According to legend, rumour had it that both Rudkin and Philpot were adversaries for some time and they both were vying for the affections of the daughter of a prominent citizen of St. John's who lived at Quidi Vidi Village.

On one occasion during a social function, Philpot was goaded into insulting Rudkin but soon afterwards apologized. On Wednesday, March 29, 1826, most of the officers of the Royal Veteran Companies gathered at the quarters of Captain Matthew Henry Willock for a party and friendly game of lanscolet, an old card game.

According to witnesses who later testified at the resulting trial, controversy arose over the ownership of a £2.8/6 pot that resulted in some exchange of words and Philpot tossing water in Rudkin's face. After repeated attempts to resolve the matter by gentlemanly means, Rudkin, according to the Laws of Honour, felt obliged to call out Philpot for his contemptuous actions.

In the early afternoon of March 30, 1826, the two men proceeded to a site about a mile from St. John's at West's Farm near Brine's Tavern at the foot of Robinson's Hill adjacent to Brine's River. Rudkin's second was Dr. James Coulter Strachan, assistant surgeon of the Royal Veteran Company, while Captain George Farquhar Morice of the HMCS Grasshopper acted as Philpot's second.

Wallis and Banks pistols were used, but while Philpot was considered a good shot, Rudkin was an expert marksman. Strachan give the signal to fire and while Philpot's shot missed its intended target, it grazed Rudkin's collar. Rudkin had fired aimlessly into the air in hope that the disagreement would be settled amicably. Philpot refused and as a result, a second round was prepared.

This time Morice gave the signal to fire, to which Philpot was mortally wounded and died soon afterwards on the field. Rudkin, agitated and confused, reported the incident to his commanding officer at Fort Townsend. Rudkin was subsequently charged with murder in the first degree, while Strachan and Morice were charged as accessories in the second degree.

The historic trial began on April 17, 1826, with Chief Justice Richard Alexander Tucker presiding. At the conclusion of the trial, the Chief Justice addressed the jury and began to give his personal feeling of the Laws of England, stating there was no "Law of Honour" in the British court system and admonishing the accused prisoners.

The jury returned with a verdict of guilty, but without malice. The Chief Justice was furious, and refused to accept the verdict. He sent the jury back to deliberate further. Twenty minutes later the jury returned with a "not guilty" verdict.

BREAKING THE BANK

The Colonial Building, built of white limestone in 1850, housed the Newfoundland legislature until 1959. This building was the scene of many historic events, including Newfoundland's first bank robbery.

According to a Heritage Newfoundland and Labrador website, Newfoundland's first bank robbery took place inside the Colonial Building where there was a savings bank in the basement. Historical records suggest that on the night of November 30, 1850, two men broke into the Newfoundland Savings Bank and stole £413.

The *Royal Gazette* reported on December 3 that "the robbers entered the office by a window which they forced open, and removed an iron chest containing the money to a lower apartment where the chest was broken open, and the above sum abstracted therefrom."

Two men, James Kavanagh and Michael Whelan, were convicted of the crime in March 1851, but only £270 of the stolen money was recovered.

HANG 'EM HIGH

The steps going up the side of the courthouse in St. John's are situated on an area once known as Market House Hill. In the 19th Century, this was an important gathering place for the people. In addition to being the grounds of the city's court, post office, and produce market, it was a center for open-air auctions and the site of the public gallows.

According to common belief, the last public hanging in Newfoundland took place on this hill in January of 1835 when a man named John Flood was executed for highway robbery.

However, St. John's historian and author, Jack Fitzgerald, disputes that claim.

In his book, "Ten Steps to the Gallows," he writes, "John Flood, a romantic local highwayman, is mistakenly credited by St. John's historians as being the last man publicly hanged in Newfoundland. Flood had been tried for highway robbery and assault. The highwayman was sentenced to be executed on January 12, 1835 which, had it been carried out, would have made him the last person publicly executed in Newfoundland and Labrador."

The reprieve of the execution order was issued on January 1, 1835. Whatever became of John Flood, if he didn't hang that day, remains a mystery.

SPEAKING OF HANGING

Eleanor Power, who died on October 11, 1754, has the dubious distinction of being the first English woman to be executed in what is known today as Canada. She was hanged for the murder of William Keen, who was a justice of the peace in St. John's at that time.

Power, her husband Robert Power, and seven other men were convicted of murdering Keen in a burglary attempt of Keen's summer home on September 9, 1754. There had been ten accomplices who initially broke into Keen's house and stole a chest and some silver spoons.

When the chest was found to contain only alcohol, Eleanor Power and one of the male accomplices left the scene. The eight who remained behind decided to make another burglary attempt. When Keen awoke in his bed during the second attempt, he was beaten by two of the accomplices with a scythe and the butt of a musket. Keen died of his injuries on September 29, 1754.

On October 8, 1754, nine of the accomplices, including Eleanor Power, were brought to trial for murder before the Court of Oyer and Terminer of Newfoundland. The tenth accomplice, Nicholas Tobin, was the only Crown witness against the nine defendants. Undefended by lawyers, the nine defendants were convicted of murder by a jury after 30 minutes of deliberation and sentenced to death by hanging.

Two of the male accomplices were executed October 10, 1754. The following day, Eleanor and Robert Power followed and became the first married couple to hang together in present-day Canada. Eleanor Power was also the first non-Native American woman to be executed by British authorities in present-day Canada.

After years of imprisonment in St. John's, the five remaining defendants were eventually pardoned on condition that they leave Newfoundland and never return.

Modern legal experts believe that Eleanor Power might have escaped execution if she had been represented by a qualified lawyer at her trial. This is because while Power could have legitimately been convicted of burglary, she was likely not guilty of murder since she had abandoned the conspirators after the first break-in and played no role in Keen's death.

The same experts have also suggested that the court that convicted the nine defendants was illegally constituted because the English law that governed the Colony of Newfoundland mandated that capital trials for offences committed in Newfoundland had to be tried by courts in England.

CATHERINE MANDEVILLE SNOW

While Eleanor Power claims her place in history as the first English woman hanged in Canada, Catherine Mandeville Snow, (c. 1793 – July 21, 1834) has the distinction of being was the last woman hanged in Newfoundland.

Born at Harbour Grace, Conception Bay, as a young woman Snow moved to Salmon Cove near Port de Grave where she took up residence with a man named John William Snow, a native of Bareneed. They were married on October 30, 1828 and their union resulted in seven children.

Their marriage was said to be an unhappy one and there were frequent fights. According to reports, Catherine would fight back and throw things at him. On the night of August 31, 1833, John Snow disappeared, and it wasn't long until neighbours began to wonder if he had been murdered.

As the rumours grew, Magistrate Robert Pinsent launched an investigation, and the general suspicion was confirmed when dried blood was discovered on John Snow's fishing stage. As a result of the probe, Catherine and her first cousin Tobias Mandeville were implicated in the murder, along with Arthur Spring, one of Snow's indentured servants.

As the pressure mounted, Catherine ran away to the woods, but eventually turned herself in to the courthouse at Harbour Grace. According to the confession, John Snow was shot while going from his boat to the stagehead, but his body was never found.

The trial took place at St. John's on January 10, 1834, and despite their confessions, all had pleaded not guilty. The attorney general told the all-male jury, "I can't prove which one fired the shot, both were present for the murder. As to Catherine Snow, there is no direct or positive evidence of her guilt. But I have a chain of circumstantial evidence to prove her guilty."

During their trial it was discovered that Snow was pregnant with her eighth child. Nevertheless, the jury returned a guilty verdict in 30 minutes and on January 31, 1834, both Arthur Spring and Tobias Mandeville were hanged. Many in Newfoundland were determined that Snow should not meet the same fate.

The governor, Thomas John Cochrane, delayed her hanging until the baby was born, but on July 21, 1834, as crowds gathered on Duckworth Street, Snow walked out on the platform. Her last words were, "I was a wretched woman, but I am as innocent of any participation in the crime of murder as an unborn child."

According to the Public Ledger, "The unhappy woman, after a few brief struggles, passed into another world."

On April 1, 2012, a re-staging of Snow's trial was held in St. John's. Approximately 400 local residents attended. Snow's modern-day defense lawyer argued, "The evidence of the affair is so prejudicial, it's impossible to extricate it from the statements ... there's no way she could have a fair trial." After hearing the evidence, the modern jury acquitted her.

FOR THE RECORD

The last execution in the Dominion of Newfoundland was carried out on May 22, 1942, when Herbert Spratt was hanged in St. John's for the murder of his girlfriend, Josephine O'Brien. Spratt beat her to death with a flat iron on St. Patrick's Day 1942 in St. John's and was sentenced to hang.

IN THE LINE OF DUTY

On November 7, 1958, RCMP Constable J. Terrence Hoey was on regular police duty when he became the first police officer to be killed in the line of duty in Newfoundland. He was killed by a shotgun blast in the small community of Botwood, Newfoundland, while he was investigating a possible murder.

Constable Hoey was born in Peterborough, Ontario. Upon graduating from RCMP training academy in Regina, Saskatchewan, he was stationed in the rural coastal town of Botwood. On that fateful day in November 1958, the 21-year-old constable, along with fellow officers was investigating a possible homicide at a Chinese diner.

According to reports following the shooting, at midnight, three officers, including Constable Hoey, called out to the owner of the restaurant but got no reply. They then crawled through a side window and reached the living quarters where they found an unlocked door heavily barricaded. Constable Hoey knocked on the wooden door and was met with a single shotgun blast.

According to the book "In the Line of Duty, The Honour Roll of the RCMP," Hoey said, "I'm shot," before falling. He died within minutes.

When reinforcements arrived, tear gas was shot into the room. The owner of the restaurant responded with several blasts, one hit the Botwood fire chief in the arm. The resulting investigation was never able to determine the reason for the standoff.

Constable Hoey's body was returned to his family in Peterborough. He was buried in St. Peter's Cemetery on November 11, 1958 with an RCMP guard of honour.

While Constable Hoey was the first RCMP officer killed in Newfoundland and Labrador in the course of his duties, the first on-duty police officer killed in the province predates him by almost 100 years. The first officer killed was Constable Jeremiah Dunn of the Newfoundland Constabulary in 1861 at Harbour Grace.

A total of 16 other police and peace officers have lost their lives while on duty in the province. Their names are listed on a memorial outside Confederation Building in St. John's. It was unveiled in September 2004.

FALLEN CONSTABLES AND PEACE OFFICERS IN THE LINE OF DUTY

- Constable Jeremiah Dunn of the Newfoundland Constabulary was on patrol in Harbour Grace on October 22, 1861, with three other officers. They told two intoxicated men to go home, but the men refused. One of the men was arrested, but a large crowd gathered as the officers tried to make the second arrest. Some threw stones and one hit Dunn in the head. He died five days later from his injuries.
- Chief Constable Charles Calpin of the Terra Nova Constabulary died on August 9, 1870, in Bay Roberts when he accidentally shot himself while putting down a dog that had bit a child.
- According to a year-end report to the House of Assembly for 1884, Sgt. Thomas Fennessey of the Newfoundland Constabulary was "accidentally smothered in the snow while doing his rounds on duty at Betts Cove, on January, 27 1884."
- Ranger Danny Corcoran of the Newfoundland Rangers was on a cross-country patrol on the Northern Peninsula in the spring of 1936, but he got lost on his return to Harbour Deep. The Rangers searched for Corcoran but didn't find him until almost a month later. He was still alive but in poor shape. Corcoran had walked, then crawled and almost made it to Harbour Deep when he fell through ice, soaking his feet, which subsequently froze. After he was found, he was taken to St. Anthony where a doctor amputated his feet and diagnosed tetanus. Corcoran died on April 7, 1936 before an anti-toxin could arrive from St. John's.
- Cpl. Michael Greene of the Newfoundland Rangers died near Lamaline in March 1939 after his horse and sled fell through the ice at Danzic Point.
- Ranger Michael Collins of the Newfoundland Rangers died on August 8, 1946 after being injured on duty in a motorcycle accident at Indian Head on the Port au Port Peninsula the evening before.
- Constable Francis P. Stamp of the Newfoundland Constabulary was a well-known boxer as well as a police officer. He was the Light Heavyweight Champion of Newfoundland in 1929. He was working the night shift in the wee hours of May 27, 1954. While attempting to arrest two American servicemen for assault on New Gower Street, one ran away. Stamp and another officer chased down the second man. After returning to the police station on Water Street, Stamp who was then 50 years old, died from a heart attack.

- On March 10, 1959, Constable William Moss of the Newfoundland Constabulary was hit on the head with a piece of pulp wood during the Badger riot, which occurred during a loggers' strike in the town. He died two days later.
- RCMP Constable Robert W. Amey and his partner, Constable David Keith, were trying to recapture four men who escaped from Her Majesty's Penitentiary in St. John's. On December 17, 1964, the men broke through a roadblock near Whitbourne in a stolen car. The men left the car and ran away and were found hiding in the town. When Amey went to radio for help, the men rushed Keith, beat him, and grabbed his service revolver. Amey drew his weapon but one of the fugitives fired three shots. One hit Amey in the chest, killing him instantly. Afterwards, Keith used Amey's gun to arrest all four men.
- On September 16, 1969, Assistant Forest Ranger Silas Baikie of the Newfoundland Department of Natural Resources died in a boating accident while on patrol at Charley's Point in Lake Melville, Labrador.
- Fishery guardians Calvin Augustus Swyers and John Young of the Department of Fisheries and Oceans (DFO) were killed in a helicopter crash near Barachois Pond Park on June 2, 1973. The two were patrolling with a civilian pilot when they were caught in an unexpected wind and rainstorm. The pilot was also killed.
- In August 1975, Forest Rangers Gary Noseworthy and Carl Francis George of the Newfoundland Department of Natural Resources were killed on forest fire patrol in Wabush, Labrador when their plane crashed.
- DFO Fishery Officer Joseph V. Tremblett was patrolling the shores of Lake Melville, Labrador on August 5, 1981, when he slipped off rocks into deep water and drowned.
- On September 18, 1957, Constable Samuel Jeffers of the Newfoundland Constabulary was in a motorcycle accident while on duty in St. John's. Jeffers never recovered from head injuries and spent 43 years at the Waterford Hospital before dying on September 4, 2000.

THE MOUNT CASHEL SCANDAL

Mount Cashel Orphanage, located in St. John's, was operated by the Congregation of Christian Brothers. The facility is remembered for a scandal and protracted court cases regarding abuse of children.

The Roman Catholic Archbishop of St. John's, Michael Francis Howley, donated land in 1898 for an orphanage on the northeastern edge of the capital. The orphanage was named the Mount Cashel Boys Home. The facility was located on the eastern side of the intersection of Mount Cashel Road and Torbay Road.

The Mount Cashel Orphanage, as with numerous other orphanages in Newfoundland, received a bequest from the estate of James M. Ryan in 1917. Following Confederation in 1949, the provincial government began to place wards of the state at the Mount Cashel Orphanage in the 1950s.

For the last 40 years of operation, the facility was operated by the Christian Brothers of Ireland in Canada (CBIC). The CBIC announced on November 27, 1989 that the orphanage would be closing.

Canada's largest sexual abuse scandal — one of the largest in the world — was disclosed in 1989. Eventually, an extensive pattern of sexual and physical abuse of more than 300 orphanage residents perpetrated by staff members, specifically members of the Christian Brothers of Ireland in Canada (CBIC), was uncovered during the late 1980s and early 1990s. This resulted in the closure of the facility in 1990 after the last resident was moved to an alternate facility.

Multiple criminal investigations, a provincial government-commissioned Royal Commission of Inquiry, known as the Hughes Inquiry, and an inquiry commissioned by the Archdiocese of St. John's known as the Winter Commission, resulted in criminal convictions and millions of dollars in court-imposed financial settlements. Compensation was provided by the Government of Newfoundland for orphanage residents who were wards of the state.

The property was seized and the site razed and sold for real-estate development in the mid-1990s as part of a court settlement ordering financial compensation to the victims. Today, a Sobeys supermarket at 10 Elizabeth Avenue and a small residential development sit on the land once occupied by the orphanage.

THE ROYAL NEWFOUNDLAND CONSTABULARY

The Royal Newfoundland Constabulary (RNC) dates back to 1729, with the appointment of the first police constables. Today, it provides policing to the communities of St. John's and the Northeast Avalon Peninsula, Corner Brook, Churchill Falls, Labrador City and Wabush.

In the 19th Century, the RNC was modelled after the Royal Irish Constabulary (RIC) when, in 1844, Timothy Mhellitc of the RIC was seconded to be Inspector General, making it the oldest civil police force in North America.

Mitchell served as Inspector General and Superintendent of Police until 1871, when the Newfoundland Constabulary was reorganized with a new Police Act.

In January 1909, John J. Sullivan became the first Newfoundland-born police chief of the RNC.

Dale Gilbert Jarvis, writing for the Heritage Foundation of Newfoundland and Labrador, says that John J. Sullivan was born in Trinity in 1846, son of Florence and Annie (Handlon) Sullivan. He was educated in St. John's, and married first Annie Donoghue, then Mary E. McCourt.

Sullivan had joined the newly-formed Newfoundland Constabulary in 1871, and was made sub-inspector by 1885. Following the St. John's Great Fire of 1892 he was named fire commissioner. He later reorganized the St. John's fire department (a division of the constabulary), while continuing to serve as second-in-command of the police.

Sullivan became acting Inspector General in 1908, and the next year was confirmed in the post. He was the first native-born head of the constabulary. Sullivan retired in 1917, a recipient of the Imperial Service Order and the King's Police Medal. He died a year later.

During the Second World War, the RNC pursued spies and criminal elements in the foreign military stationed at St. John's. In 1979, Queen Elizabeth II conferred the designation "Royal" on the Newfoundland Constabulary, in recognition of its long history of service to Newfoundland and Labrador.

THE FIRST OF HER KIND

Lawyer Louise Saunders was called to the bar in 1933 and went on to become the first woman lawyer in Newfoundland. She began her career as a legal secretary in the office of Richard Squires, who was Prime Minister of Newfoundland during the 1920s. Saunders was born in Greenspond in 1893 and died in St. John's in 1969.

FIVE FAST FACTS

1 The St. John's Electric Light Company built the colony's first generating station in 1885. Known as the Flavin Lane Station, it was built for the Terra Nova Bakery located at 11 Water Street.

2 A carelessly dropped pipe, a stable full of hay and a poorly-time closure of the city's water supply culminated in the Great Fire of 1892. The inferno raged through St. John's, destroying most of the city and leaving more than 11,000 homeless.

3 The first mail and passenger train crossed Newfoundland from St. John's to Port-aux-Basques in June 1898. The last passenger train ran the line in 1969, while the last freight train made the run in 1988.

4 Guglielmo Marconi successfully received the first transatlantic radio signal on Signal Hill in St. John's on December 12, 1901. It was sent from Ireland, some 3,400 km across the Atlantic Ocean, and it proved that radio waves would follow the curvature of the Earth.

5 On the night of April 14, 1912, the wireless station in Cape Race, located on the southern tip of the Avalon Peninsula received a distress signal from the doomed ocean liner *Titanic*, which had struck an iceberg 600 km off Newfoundland's southeast coast.

LEGENDS, GHOST STORIES AND SUPERSTITIONS

SHEILA'S BRUSH

For generations, people in Newfoundland and Labrador have had a particular name for a storm that comes on the heels of St. Patrick's Day.

As everyone in Newfoundland knows, winter is not over until Sheila's Brush arrives with a vengeance.

Sheila's Brush in Newfoundland folklore is a winter storm that occurs after St. Patrick's Day and is always thought of as the end to winter. No one seems to know with certainty of Sheila's relationship to St. Patrick. Some say she was his wife or mistress, others insist that she was his mother, sister or even his housekeeper, yet there does seem to have been some connection between the two.

Another uncertainty is with the time of the storm. It could happen on March 17th or it might not be here until late April and has even been known to stay away until May.

The one absolute is that Sheila and her brush will arrive. Some Newfoundland fishermen are so convinced of this that they will not head out to sea until the storm has come and gone.

THE OLD HAG OF NEWFOUNDLAND

Legend has it that it happens when all things dark and evil happen — the middle of the night, naturally.

And it happens when what you thought was a peaceful night's sleep turns into a waking nightmare as you find yourself pinned and unable to move, shocked awake and paralyzed by an overwhelming sense of evil. In some places, but especially in Newfoundland, they say when that happens, it means the old hag has paid you a visit.

While some skeptics quickly dismiss the phenomena as your typical, everyday urban legend, the curious thing about the "Old Hag Syndrome" is that it is a highly reported phenomenon from around the world, suggesting there is more to this story than your typical superstition or old wives' tale.

Down through the generations, there have been countless reports from people around the world who have claimed, at one time or another, to have woken up in terror, paralyzed. However, their reports not only include sleep paralysis, but they also often report seeing or hearing strange things, such as eyes in the darkness or the heavy sound of footsteps. Some witnesses also report seeing a dark figure looming over their bodies.

The story of the Old Hag finds its origins in folklore, particularly in Newfoundland, though variations of the story are present throughout the world. Tales tell of an old witch maliciously sitting on the chests of her victims while they lay in bed, or curses placed upon unsuspecting individuals causing them to meet this terror in the night.

It goes without saying that the curse could still be an actual case of sleep paralysis, which typically occurs when entering or coming out of REM sleep. A person may become "caught" in a state between sleep and consciousness, during which they remain aware of their surroundings, but are unable to move. Furthermore, it's true that the prevailing sense of evil, or the alleged noises, that accompany the "Old Hag" could be nothing more than hallucinations occurring in that state of half-dreaming.

However, that does not explain the people who have reported similar experiences *without* the paralysis? The commonality of every reporting? And why, of all the possible hallucinations we could experience, do we sense evil?

Scientists and paranormal enthusiasts may be at odds about what causes the Old Hag Syndrome, but one simple truth may be enough to keep you up at night — whatever the cause, it *does* exist.

The existence of the Old Hag legend in itself isn't all that strange as it sounds like Bloody Mary or any other urban legend. But what really distinguishes this legend from the rest is the associations with witchcraft and curses. Whatever the cause, the Old Hag legend seems to be deeply rooted into Newfoundland's rich and varied culture.

MUMMERING

The Christmas-time tradition of house visiting that takes place in Newfoundland and Labrador, is known as Mummering. It also occurs in isolated regions of Ireland, especially in Fingal.

Also known as Mumming or Janneying, the tradition usually involves a group of friends or family who dress in disguise and visit homes within their community or neighbouring communities during the 12 days of Christmas. If the mummers are welcomed into a house, they often do a variety of informal performances that may include dance, music, jokes, or recitations.

The hosts must guess the mummers' identities before offering them food or drink. They may poke and prod the mummers or ask them questions. To make this a challenge for the hosts, the mummers may stuff their costumes, cross-dress, or speak while inhaling. Once the mummers have been identified, they remove their disguises, spend some social time with the hosts, and then travel as a group to the next home.

An old Christmas custom from England and Ireland, mummering, in a version of its modern form, can be traced back in Newfoundland into the 19th Century. Although it is unclear precisely when this tradition was brought to Newfoundland by the English and Irish, the earliest record dates back to 1819. The tradition varied, and continues to vary, from community to community. Some formal aspects of the tradition, such as the mummers play have largely died out, with the informal house visiting remaining the predominant form.

On June 25, 1861, an "Act to make further provisions for the prevention of Nuisances" was introduced in response to the death of Issac Mercer in Bay Roberts, Newfoundland. Mercer had been murdered by a group of masked mummers on December 28, 1860. The Bill made it illegal to wear a disguise in public without permission of the local magistrate. Mummering in rural communities continued despite the passage of the Bill, although the practice did die out in larger towns and cities.

In 2009, the Heritage Foundation of Newfound and Labrador's Intangible Cultural Heritage office established what would become an annual Mummers Festival, culminating in a Mummers Parade in St. John's. The success of the festival has influenced, in part, another revitalization and increase of interest in the tradition in the province.

THE VIKING GHOST SHIP

This ghostly tale spans three centuries, with reports that reach from Newfoundland to Iceland.

According to archaeological data, Vikings inhabited L'Anse aux Meadows, at the northern tip of Newfoundland, for a short time around A.D. 1000. Now the only signs that the Vikings ever inhabited L'Anse aux Meadows are the archaeological remnants they left behind. But spine-tingling reports suggest the spirits of the Vikings have been travelling the seas towards Newfoundland for centuries.

These sightings always occur in early June and the reports claim that a ghostly Viking vessel has been reportedly seen sailing by the southwest coast of Iceland. Approximately 20 days later, Newfoundlanders are reported to have seen the eerie vessel and heard its horn blowing late at night off the coast of L'Anse aux Meadows.

Could it be that these early inhabitants are returning to claim what they've left behind?

THE HAG OF BELL ISLAND

A "banshee" is believed to wander the Dobbin's Garden area and the surrounding marshland on Bell Island.

According to Irish folklore, banshees are messengers of impending death. Legend suggests that their cries signal that a loved one will soon die. They are reported to appear in two forms — as a beautiful woman dressed in white or as a frightening old hag. In most accounts, the banshee that inhabits Bell Island is of the latter variety.

Local legend holds that men who have gone near the area have mysteriously gone missing for days at a time. When they finally emerge from the marshland, they are completely unaware of the time that has lapsed. In fact, their only memory of the event is of a foul odour and, most often, a deformed old woman forcing them to the ground.

VICTORIA STREET VISITORS

According to local legend and stories that have been passed down through the generations, Victoria Street in St. John's is widely accepted as Newfoundland's most haunted Street.

One of the oldest Streets in the city, it is the location of the historic LSPU Hall, the longtime hub of theatre and music in the city. In recent years, a phantom has been spotted at the building, sometimes taking in a show at the theatre.

It has also been reported that another harmless spirit haunts 23 Victoria Street, and still other, more frightening spirits, have been reported at a house near the corner of Victoria and Bond Streets. At this location, during the winter of 1907-1908, a woman awoke to a horrific scene — a ghostly female figure dragging another female spirit along the floor by her hair.

NEWFOUNDLAND'S OWN LOCH NESS MONSTER

According to residents of Robert's Arm, Newfoundland, a monster lives in Crescent Lake.

Named "Cressie," locals have been sighting the beast, reportedly as long as 40 feet, since the turn of the century.

In the early 1980s, a huge hole appeared in the ice covering the lake. With no reasonable explanation for this phenomenon, residents believed that Cressie was the most likely culprit.

DEVIL'S HAND

The small town of Fortune Harbour, Notre Dame Bay, was once the scene of a very bizarre card game.

A man named Kincheler loved his game dearly and he often bragged how nothing could sway him from a game of cards. One night Kincheler walked three miles to play a game, boasting to his fellows there that he would have a game of cards with the devil himself.

After the game was over and Kincheler left to walk home, he met up with a stranger who struck up a conversation with Kincheler. The mysterious man said he, too, loved cards and challenged Kincheler to a game, and of course, the eager man agreed.

The two played for hours and as the mysterious stranger began to become visibly angry, Kincheler noticed a twitching tail coming from under the coat of the now fuming stranger. Kincheler laid his winning card and with that the stranger slammed his last card down upon the rock on which they were playing.

Kincheler won his card game but the hand print of that mysterious man is still seen on that rock today.

The devil hates to lose...

THE PIRATE TREASURE OF TORBAY

Like many Newfoundland communities today, the small place near Torbay known as Tapper's Cove once had a different name.

Originally called Treasure Cove, the stream found there was allegedly built by pirates. The stream had a wooden bottom which hid the gold that the pirates had stolen from other pirates who plundered it from a Spanish galleon in the 17th Century. The pirates who had originally stolen the gold were attacked and driven into the hills of Torbay by the second lot, who then built the stream to hide the gold.

To protect their treasure, the pirates kidnapped a young boy and his Newfoundland dog from Torbay and killed them, believing their ghosts would guard their hidden treasure. To this day, people steer clear of Tapper's Cove after dark, afraid of meeting the ghosts of the headless boy and his spectral Newfoundland dog who restlessly guard their charges.

THE MYSTERY OF THE *RESOLVEN*

The British gunboat, the Mallard, found the *Resolven* floating on the open sea near Catalina, Newfoundland in 1884. The *Resolven* had left Harbour Grace, Newfoundland bound for Labrador with a cargo of salt and four Newfoundland passengers only a few days earlier, on August 27, 1884.

When the crew of the Mallard signaled the other boat, they received no response and so proceeded to board her. What the British sailors found there was a complete mystery. The *Resolven* held no passengers. Clothing and other personal items were found undisturbed on the ship and there was absolutely no sign of trouble. The galley held a set table ready for a meal and a fire still burned in the stove.

The surrounding water was searched but no sign of the crew or passengers was ever to be found.

THE KNOCKING OF FORAN'S HOTEL

During one cold dark winter night, the guests of Foran's Hotel in downtown St. John's were awakened to an incessant knocking coming from an upstairs room. Upon entering the room, the loud knocking suddenly ceased and although two men searched the room, they could find no explanation for the noise.

The noise resumed each night and would continue until someone entered the room. Word of the strange knocking spread quickly through the community and people believed the old hotel to be haunted.

This occurred until six months after the initial event when a stranger came one night and was given the haunted room. Not knowing of the strange knocking, the stranger entered the room and all was quiet until midnight when the noise began again, louder and more horrifying than before.

The knocking filled the building until the door to the room was finally opened, only to reveal the stranger lying dead on the floor, a look of total terror covering his face. The knocking occurred for the last time while the body was being removed from the room.

The old Foran's Hotel has been torn down since then, being replaced by the General Post Office on Water Street but people are still wary of being alone there after dark, afraid the knocking may once more be heard...

THE CRY

William Welsh lived in 18th Century St. John's, Newfoundland with his wife and three sons.

Like many Newfoundlanders at the time, the Welsh family had strong ties to the old land. Welsh's ancestors came from Ireland and had a strong belief in Irish traditions and folklore, as did William's wife and sons, although the businessman himself did not.

One night, Mrs. Welsh was sitting in bed when she became frozen in fear of what she heard. It was an unearthly wail that came slowly closer to the window until it sounded like it was outside. Then the wail became a wild shriek, dying away in a horrifying sobbing.

William Welsh never heard a thing and dismissed it as her imagination, until his son cut an artery the next day and came close to dying. The unnatural cry was never mentioned again until many years later, at William Welsh's 60th birthday party which boasted some of the most important citizens of St. John's.

Suddenly the door burst open and Welsh's eldest son stood there, a look of horror on his face. He asked his father if he was okay, saying he heard the cry once again, leaving the other guests standing around in wonder. William Welsh laughed it off as silly superstition, telling the guests the story of his Irish tradition and continued with his party.

William Welsh suddenly died at breakfast the next day, finally believing in the mournful cry of the Banshee...

SUPERSTITIONS

In Newfoundland and Labrador, it is bad luck to ...
- put new shoes on the table.
- whistle on a boat.
- have a bird fly into your house.
- fall up a set of steps.
- walk over someone as it will stunt their growth.
- break a mirror. (If you do, you'll have seven years bad luck.)
- pass another person on the stairs.
- put your keys on the table.
- walk under a ladder.
- have 13 people sit at the table.

- drop a deck of cards.
- coil a rope against the sun.
- purchase a new broom in May.
- lean a broom against a bed.
- sweep dirt out the front door.
- sweep the floor after the sun goes down.
- put a hat on the bed.
- meet a red haired woman at your front door.
- look over another person's shoulder and into a mirror.
- enter a building by one door and exit by using another.
- spill salt.
- cross knives on a table.
- leave a knife turned blade upwards.
- have a lone black crow fly over your head.
- be called back just as you have begun a journey.
- have the groom see the bride before the ceremony.
- drop the ring at a marriage ceremony.
- find a spider in your drinking glass.

It is good luck to …
- see the new moon first over the left shoulder.
- pick up a horseshoe on the road.
- pick a four-leaf clover.
- see two black crows flying overhead.
- put on a garment inside out by mistake.
- pick up a penny from the ground.
- pick up a pin or a white button from the ground.
- hear a rooster crow on the doorstep.
- see a baby smiling in its sleep.
- dream of one's father.
- find a ladybug in your home.
- put on odd coloured socks.
- wear a sock with a hole in it.
- toss salt over your left shoulder.

- break a lace while tying your shoe.
- say "God Bless Me" when you sneeze.
- step onto a boat by putting your right foot first.
- knock on wood three times.
- take a cat onboard a boat.
- leave the last mouthful of rum in the bottle.
- find two egg yolks inside one shell.
- find nine peas in a pea pod.
- find a cricket in your house.
- see three butterflies together.

SIGNS OF DEATH

In Newfoundland and Labrador, to hear the banshee crying at night is said to precede the death of certain persons of Irish descent, or when rigor mortis does not appear in a corpse it means that another member of the family will soon die.

Other sings of death include …

- a dog moaning near a house.
- a dog burying an object near one's home.
- a bird coming into the house.
- a bird hitting a window.
- a clock which had been stopped for years suddenly striking the hours.
- a window blind falling without any apparent cause.
- a window slamming closed on its own.
- a picture suddenly falling from the wall.
- dreaming of a wedding.
- hearing three knocks at your door yet there is no one there.

OFF TO SEA

The sea is a dangerous place, and seafaring men have invented countless superstitions to keep them safe until they are back on dry land. As would be expected, there are many superstitions coming from Newfoundland and Labrador that originate from the sea, such as:

- Having a woman on board, distracting the sailors, is thought to bring terrible luck on a crew. However, a naked woman is said to calm stormy seas, which explains the busty figureheads found on the front of ships.
- The most unlikely nautical superstition claims that bananas on board spell disaster. One theory dates back to the 17th Century when slave ships sometimes travelled with a cargo of bananas. The fruit was known to release deadly methane gas into the hold, suffocating African slaves trapped inside.
- Having someone on board with mittens that were not white could send a captain back to shore to begin a voyage again, that is, after the coloured mittens were disposed of.
- They say that every time a sea gull cries another fisherman dies somewhere in the world.
- Come aboard a ship with your right foot first for good luck. You're also less prone to injury.
- It is considered bad luck for shipbuilders to be on board during the vessel's maiden voyage.
- If you could skip a rock through the crest of a wave you would be able to cut the devil's throat.
- Fishermen and sailors consider it good luck to see dolphins swimming next to their vessel, but a shark following a ship is a sign of death.
- Never change the name of a vessel once it's been christened as it is bad luck.
- It is unlucky to kill a gull as they are said to possess the souls of dead sailors.
- Ship builders place a silver coin under the masthead to bring the vessel good luck.
- It is bad luck to wish good luck to someone heading out to sea.
- In some Maritime communities it is considered bad luck to take a woman fishing with you because they keep the fish from biting.
- Whistling is not permitted because it is said to bring on a storm. Only two people can whistle on a ship — the captain because he knows how to control the wind and the cook because it is impossible to whistle while you're chewing and if the cook is whistling then he isn't eating. Any crewmember heard whistling will be asked to leave the ship.
- You never leave port on a Friday because it means you will have a bad trip. Most times ships would either depart no later than 11:59 p.m. on Thursday and no earlier than 12:01 a.m. on Saturday.
- It is bad luck to turn anything upside down on a ship because it simulates capsizing. You're not even to open a can upside down. It's so bad that some sailors and fishermen won't even do that when they're on land.

- You never ring a bell unnecessarily on board a ship because it means a sailor somewhere it going to die. On most ships, they keep the bell wrapped in cloth and the clapper is kept secured. They only ring the bell when the occasion calls for it.
- You must never bring an umbrella on deck as it suggests that there will be a rainstorm and you don't want that when you're at sea.
- You must never wear black socks on board a ship because black is the colour of death and that could spell disaster for your voyage. It's okay to wear white, khaki, grey or navy, but never black.
- Always put a coin under the ship's mast to pay the ferryman when crossing the River Styx. This stems from the Bible and whenever we change the mast on Bluenose, we also place a special coin there.
- You cannot say "pig" on board a ship. Now that's because pigs have cloves and hoofs and that supposedly reminds people of the Devil.
- Whenever any alcoholic beverage is served on board a ship, before anyone else has a drink you must offer a drink to Neptune and offer a drink to the ship's deck.
- It is bad luck to stick a knife in the mast because it will bring on a big wind.
- It is bad luck to have 13 characters in the name of a ship.
- It is good luck to have A in the name of a ship, especially three As.
- It is bad luck to leave a hatch upside down because it could result in the ship being turned over.
- It is bad luck to have a total of 13 members in a ship's crew.
- When going aloft, it is bad luck to pass through the shrouds leading to the ratlines.
- One must always go around the shrouds, fore or aft, but never through them.
- It is bad luck to pee off the deck of a ship into the ocean.
- Spitting into the ocean can break a spell of bad luck.
- It is bad luck to bring a red-headed person on board a ship.

FIVE FAST FACTS

1   A referendum held in 1915 on the total prohibition of the sale and consumption of alcohol received about 5,000 votes, number needed to enact the ban. Prohibition became law on January 1, 1917 and remained in force until 1924, after which a quota system for purchasing alcoholic drinks was introduced. The system was scrapped on March 31, 1966.

2   At around 1:45 p.m. on June 14, 1919, John Alcock and Arthur Whitten Brown left St. John's and flew 3,041.7 km in just under 16 and a half hours to land in Clifden, Ireland, to complete the first flight across the Atlantic Ocean.

3   Newfoundland became Canada's tenth province on March 31, 1949.

4   After seven years and nearly a billion dollars, the electric power station at Churchill Falls was completed in 1972.

5   The Hibernia oilfield is identified in 1979 off the Grand Banks. It is the fifth largest discovered in Canada.

An empty oil tanker near the Newfoundland shore.

POLITICS

THE BIRTH OF A PROVINCE

Newfoundland and Labrador's political and legal history got off to a rocky start.

Viewing settlement as an impediment to the all-important fishery, Britain was not concerned with the colony's law and governance. Instead, for decades, the colony was "governed" by the Fishing Admiral system. The captain of the first ship to drop anchor in any harbour each spring earned the right to be the Fishing Admiral and become the governor for the season.

Regardless of his legal training or education, the makeshift governor was empowered to act as judge and jury. He decided all legal matters, though not with impartiality. Decisions frequently supported his interests and major offences went unpunished.

Officials recognized that the system was not working. Although only a slight improvement, King William's Act of 1699 dictated that the commodore of the annual naval fleet would act as governor each year throughout his tenure. There was no longer a new leader each spring, but the fishery, not law and order, remained the top priority. As inadequate and ineffectual as it was, this form of governance remained in effect through the 18th Century, as settlements were established and grew.

RESPONSIBLE GOVERNMENT

In the early 19th Century, Newfoundlanders, egged on by enlightened European immigrants, called for the right to elect their lawmakers in a system of representative government. The colony got its wish in 1832, although executive powers remained with the Crown.

Before long, Newfoundlanders were dissatisfied with the limited form of this representative government. Newfoundland's governing elite — merchants and entrepreneurs who seemed to care more for their own industry than the future of the colony — were accused of negatively impacting the colony's political evolution. Religious strife was thrown into the mix, with appointed officials almost always belonging to the Church of England, while many of the elected representatives were Roman Catholic.

Elected officials, and those who put them there, wanted more. They wanted the independence that came with colonial status. In 1855, after several tense and violence- riddled decades, Britain granted Newfoundland responsible government. The colony's executive became "responsible" and they were chosen from elected members of the House of Assembly, and were answerable to the public's electoral endorsement.

Newfoundland became an independent, self-governing dominion on September 26, 1907, the same day the colony of New Zealand won its independence.

When New Brunswick, Nova Scotia, and the colonies of Upper and Lower Canada were discussing union, Newfoundland was also invited to join. But when the first four provinces struck their deal in 1867, Newfoundland wanted no part of it. The possibility of confederation, however, never completely left the agenda.

CONFEDERATION

Between 1864 and 1949, the debate resurfaced several times, especially as the colony-cum-dominion faced financial hardships. In 1869, anti-confederates won the first Confederation election, convincing Newfoundlanders they could prosper without the support of Canada.

Events of the 1930s conspired to make Confederation a more attractive prospect. That decade's Great Depression ravaged the Island's economy much as it did elsewhere in North America. In 1934, Newfoundland's system of responsible government collapsed along with the economy. In return for Britain's financial support, Newfoundland surrendered her governance to a British-appointed commission of seven for a Commission of Government.

For 15 years, no elections were held and no legislature convened. It was into this political abyss that the issue of Confederation re-emerged in the late 1940s. Although coy about its intentions, Canada was interested in Newfoundland and had the support of both Britain and a fiery and persuasive Newfoundlander named Joseph R. Smallwood.

In 1948, Newfoundlanders had to choose their political future from three options,

- Return to responsible government as it existed in the years leading up to 1934
- Join the Confederation of Canada
- Continue with the Commission of Government.

Following a series of referendums, Newfoundlanders narrowly voted to join Confederation. On March 31, 1949, Newfoundlanders became Canadian citizens.

The vote in favour of Confederation was narrow — when the final numbers were tallied, just 52 percent had voted in favour. Many of the remaining 48 percent refused to accept the results. Anti-Confederaters were led by Peter Cashin, who called the deal an "unholy union" between London and Ottawa. To protest the union, on April 1, 1949, anti-Confederates raised black flags and wore black armbands of disapproval.

To this day, conspiracy theorists contend Newfoundlanders were duped, and that in order to ensure Joey Smallwood's Confederation dream, the vote were switched and the majority "yes" votes were actually "no" votes. Many people believe that federal jurisdiction over important industries such as fishing and offshore oil has inhibited the province's ability to manage its own affairs.

Newfoundland's main source of pre-1949 custom duties also fell under federal jurisdiction, while the financially heft responsibilities of health care, social services and education were given to the province.

Premiers of Newfoundland and Labrador since joining Confederation

- Joey Smallwood (Liberal), April 1, 1949 – January 18, 1972
- Frank Moores (Progressive Conservative), January 18, 1972 – March 26, 1979
- Brian Peckford (Progressive Conservative), March 26, 1979 – March 22, 1989
- Tom Rideout (Progressive Conservative), March 22, 1989 – May 5, 1989
- Clyde Wells (Liberal), May 5, 1989 – January 26, 1996
- Brian Tobin (Liberal), January 26, 1996 – October 16, 2000
- Beaton Tulk (Liberal), October 16, 2000 – February 13, 2001
- Roger Grimes (Liberal), February 13, 2001 – November 6, 2003
- Danny Williams (Progressive Conservative), November 6, 2003 – December 3, 2010
- Kathy Dunderdale (Progressive Conservative), December 3, 2010 – January 24, 2014
- Tom Marshall (Progressive Conservative), January 24, 2014 – September 26, 2014
- Paul Davis (Progressive Conservative), September 26, 2014 – December 14, 2015
- Dwight Ball (Liberal), December 14, 2015 –

THE LITTLE MAN FROM GAMBO

Newfoundland and Labrador's most loved and loathed politician, Joseph R. (Joey) Smallwood, was born on Christmas Eve, 1900, in the small community of Gambo.

Smallwood got an early taste of public life as a newspaper apprentice. Interested in publishing and a life off the Island, a bespectacled 20-year-old Joey left for New York. During his five years in the city he met his wife Clara and worked for a socialist newspaper. This work gave him a powerful affinity for unions and workers' rights, and when he came home in 1925, he became a vociferous union organizer and publisher.

In 1928, Smallwood entered politics as campaign manager for Liberal Richard Squires. Squires' win earned Smallwood an appointment as a justice of the peace. Fully steeped in Liberal politics, Smallwood started the Liberal newspaper, The Watchdog. Through the 1930s he was undeterred by his own electoral losses and continued to advise Liberals in the legislature.

Hi bided his time for a decade and embraced extra-political interests — he continued to organize labour, became a broadcaster with his own radio show, From the Masthead, and established a pig farm. By 1946, Smallwood was a well-known figure in Newfoundland. He used his notoriety and his access to the airwaves to promote a cause near and dear to his heart — and that cause was Confederation.

First Premier of Canada's newest province

Smallwood's belief that Confederation would bring prosperity to Newfoundland struck an appealing chord with many cash-strapped Newfoundlanders. In the 1948 provincial referendum, a small majority voted to join Canada and Smallwood became the first Liberal Premier of Canada's tenth province. For almost a quarter of century, he ran the government of Newfoundland, some say with autocratic control over the economy and media.

Smallwood's critics charge that over time he became more interested in his own legacy than with the well-being of Newfoundland. Many have condemned his decision to relocate outport communities, while others have criticized him for abandoning workers' rights in favour of big business. He brushed off such criticisms and staunchly maintained that the economic and social development of Newfoundland was his top priority.

As proof, he offered a host of projects completed during his tenure. Roads and electric grids were established, Memorial University became a degree-granting institution, and his brainchild — The Encyclopaedia of Newfoundland and Labrador — chronicled the province's history in unprecedented depth.

Despite the fact that he had resigned from Smallwood's cabinet because of his leader's authoritarianism, former premier Clyde Wells once asserted that Smallwood was "perhaps the greatest Newfoundlander that ever lived." While many Newfoundlanders and Labradorians would agree, probably an equal number would not. Regardless, it is undeniable that "the little man from Gambo" forever changed Newfoundland and Labrador.

Smallwood died on December 17, 1991, in St. John's at the age of 90.

FIVE FAST FACTS

1 An official amendment to the Constitution of Canada in 2001 officially changed the name of the province to Newfoundland and Labrador.

2 At the 2006 Olympic Games in Turin, Italy, skip Brad Gushue, a 25-year-old Newfoundlander, led the Canadian men's curling team (with second Russ Howard, third Mark Nichols, and lead Jamie Korab) to its first-ever Olympic curling gold — the first Newfoundland and Labrador-based athletes to win the top Olympic medal.

3 Kathy Dunderdale was sworn in as the province's tenth premier in 2010. She was the first woman to lead Newfoundland and Labrador, and easily defeated her opponents in the 2011 election. She resigned in 2014 amid criticism of her policies and leadership style.

4 In 2011, Conservative Peter Penashue became the first Labrador Innu elected to the Canadian House of Commons. He resigns in 2013.

5 The town of Bonavista is where John Cabot first laid his eyes on Newfoundland and reportedly explained, "Oh, Happy Sight" or in his native Italian, "Oh Buono Vista." A windy and barren locale, Bonavista is nevertheless quite close to important fishing and sealing grounds, so it became the place to fish for the Spanish, Portuguese, French and English during the 1500s.

TRANSPORTATION

PLANES, TRAINS AND AUTOMOBILES

Construction on the Gander International Airport, one of the first in the province, began in 1936 and by the end of 1937, the airfield had four paved runways, making it the largest airport in the world at the time.

The first airplane landed at Gander on January 11, 1938. It was a Fox Moth VO-ADE, operated by Imperial Airways for the Newfoundland Government and flown by Captain Douglas Fraser.

According to the airport's official history, by the outbreak of the Second World War in September 1939, Gander was ready for civil operations. The value of a functioning airport in such a strategic position was unique.

Gander was the only operative airport in Atlantic Canada and ultimately the airport became the main staging point for the movement of Allied aircraft to Europe during the Second World War. Gander's location on the Great Circle Route made it an ideal wartime refueling and maintenance depot for bombers flying overseas.

In November 1940, Captain D.C.T. Bennett left Gander for Europe, leading the first fleet of seven Lockheed Hudson bombers across the Atlantic during the Battle of Britain. More than 20,000 North American-built fighters and heavy bombers would follow.

In 1942, the Newfoundland Government handed over the control of the airport to the Canadian Government and it became a military airfield, with a continuous delivery of planes to the war zone.

In 1945, the Newfoundland government took over control of the airport again. By the end of the year, Pan-American World Airways, Trans-World Airline, Trans Canada Airlines (later Air Canada), and British Overseas Airway Corporation (later British Airways) began regular Atlantic air service through Gander. Gander handled 13,000 aircraft annually and a quarter million passengers, requiring a new $3 million terminal to be built and opened in June 19, 1959.

By the 1950s, Gander airport was one of the busiest international airports in the world, buoyed by transoceanic traffic.

St. John's entered the province's aviation history by 1940 when the Canadian Government agreed to construct an air base near the city. A site was chosen near the community of Torbay, against the advice of local experts who preferred Cochrane Pond, to accommodate Royal Canadian Air Force (RCAF) operations.

ST. JOHN'S AIRPORT

Construction on the runway began in 1941. At a cost of approximately 1.5 million dollars, two runways, taxiways, aprons, hangars and other facilities were built and in operation by the end of 1941. The RCAF officially opened Torbay Airport on December 15, 1941. The RCAF, Royal Air Force (RAF), and the United States Army Air Corps jointly used it until December 1946.

According to the official history of the St. John's International Airport on its corporate information website, on October 18, 1941, three American B-17 Flying Fortresses and one RCAF Digby made the first unofficial landing on the only serviceable runway available. Later that month, a British Overseas Airways Corporation B-24 Liberator en route from Prestwick, Scotland, to Gander, made the first officially sanctioned landing during a weather emergency.

November 1941 saw the arrival of No. 11 Bomber Reconnaissance (BR) Squadron, the first RCAF Squadron to take up duties at the Torbay Air Base. Additional RCAF support arrived before the end of 1942.

In April of that year, Lysander aircraft of No. 5 Coastal Artillery Co-operation Flight, which was later renamed No. 1 Composite Detachment in July 1943, took up duties at Torbay. Until its disbandment in June 1945, the Flight busied itself with search and rescue, target towing, photo reconnaissance, blackout observation, dive bomb and machine gun practice, mail drops, and once late in December 1944, a turkey drop over an RCAF radar site on Allan's Island on Newfoundland's south coast.

The airport became a civilian operation under the jurisdiction of the Canadian Department of Transport on April 1, 1946. Confusion was caused by the presence of American military personnel at a civilian airport and consequently on April 1, 1953, control was turned back to the Department of National Defence.

The Transport Department maintained control over the terminal building, a small wooden structure, which was constructed in 1943, but the facility remained RCAF Station Torbay until April 1, 1964, when it was returned to the jurisdiction of the Transport Department under the name St. John's Airport.

The control tower originally constructed during the war burned down in an extensive fire at the airport on March 17, 1946, which caused one and a half million dollars worth of damage. Construction did not begin on a new tower until 1951. It was then opened in June 1952. A new Tower/Communications Building replaced that structure in March 1976. The tower was equipped with radio navigation and landing aids including precision approach radar, non-directional beacon and VHF omni-directional range.

The first commercial air service at the facility went into operation on May 1, 1942, with the arrival at Torbay of a Trans-Canada Airlines (T.C.A.) Lockheed Lodestar aircraft with five passengers and a three-member crew on board. T.C.A. had not wanted to provide the service to St. John's because they thought it would not be economically viable. It was only after a United States company showed interest in operating the service that T.C.A. agreed to do it.

Air Canada, the successor of T.C.A., and Eastern Provincial Airways were the major airlines operating out of St. John's Airport in 1981. They provided daily service to other parts of Newfoundland and Labrador and to mainland Canada.

St. John's International Airport's strong military ties continue to the present day. Though it operates as a civilian airport, moving close to 1.5 million passengers per year, approximately 1,300 military aircraft stop at this airport each year to refuel or for crew rests.

TRAINS

By the early 20th Century, trains began to rival sailing as the dominant mode of transportation in Newfoundland. Work had started on the trans-Island Newfoundland Railing in the late 1800s. In time, the railway's passenger train would come to be affectionately known as the "Newfie Bullet" a cheerful reference to the fact it could take up to three days to cross the Island.

To save money, the tracks were laid to a narrow gauge. As a result, when goods were exported to the mainland, the train wheels had to be changed to accommodate the wider standard track. Although the 1949 terms of Confederation promised the maintenance of railroads in perpetuity, the railway has now been phased out, and the railbed has become the Trailway, a 900-km-long park.

The first freight trains started travelling the province in 1881 and the first passenger train went into service in 1898. By the early 1900s, a total of 1,458 kilometers of rail rain through the province. Passenger train service in Newfoundland and Labrador ended in July 1969, while freight train services continued until 1988 when the last train was taken off line.

AUTOMOBILES

The first automobiles arrived in Newfoundland in 1903.

While other Canadian provinces had already made the switch, drivers in Newfoundland switched to the right side of the road in 1949. Between 1949 and 1968, the number of motor vehicles in the province increased by 900 percent.

Also during the same period, paved roads increased from 194 km to 1,868 km. Today, there are 6,995 km of paved roads in Newfoundland, representing approximately 78 percent of the total number of roads in the province.

FIVE FAST FACTS

1 The final battle of the Seven Years' War in North America was fought in 1762 at the Battle of Signal Hill, in which the French surrendered St. John's to a British force under the command of Lt. Colonel William Amherst. Lt. Colonel Amherst renamed what was then known as "The Lookout" to "Signal Hill," because of the signaling that took place upon its summit from its flagmast. Flag communication between land and sea would take place there from the 17th Century until 1960.

2 The Newman Wine Vaults are the only existing historic wine vault in Newfoundland and Labrador. Located at 436 Water Street, inside one of St. John's oldest buildings, the wine port is a Provincial Historic Site.

3 Newfoundland experiences more fog than any of the other Atlantic Provinces, and part of the province is considered the foggiest place in the world.

4 St. John's is the capital of Newfoundland and Labrador. It is also the oldest city in North America and Water Street is the oldest Street in North America. Incorporated as a city in 1921, St. John's is located on the northeastern arm of the Avalon Peninsula and is the easternmost city in North America.

5 The first permanent residence in the province was established in 1528.

Row of houses in the city of Saint John's.

GLOSSARY OF NAMES

A

RCMP Constable Robert W. Amey 142
John Murray Anderson 64

B

Assistant Forest Ranger Silas Baikie 142
Captain Bob Bartlett 69
Eric Bowring 26

C

John Cabot 10, 15, 24, 106, 112, 117, 121, 132, 164
Chief Constable Charles Calpin 141
Sarah Canning 56
Bill Clark 63
Michael Coady 65
Ranger Michael Collins 141
Ranger Danny Corcoran 141
Mark Critch 60

D

Helen Frances Theresa Delaney 61
John Delany 25
Marquis de la Rade 111
Alan Doyle 59
Damhnait Doyle 70
Glen Gregory Doyle 67
Shawn Doyle 57
Kathleen "Kathy" Dunderdale 77, 161, 164
Constable Jeremiah Dunn 140
Karyn Dwyer 59
Gwynne Dyer 63

E

Amelia Mary Earhart 26, 77
Peter Easton 75, 108, 109

F

Sgt. Thomas Fennessey 141
John Flood 117, 137
Kimberly French 65
Varick Frissell 27

G

Carl Francis George 142
Jack Goodwin 24
Walter Gray 24, 45
Cpl. Michael Greene 141
Brad Gushue 164

H

Jennifer Hale 56
Allan Hawco 58
Natasha Henstridge 55
RCMP Constable J. Terrence Hoey 140
Ruby Holbrook 61
Edith Weeks Hooper 77
Robert Hunston 24, 45
Ron Hynes 70

I

Anne Stine Ingstad 103
Helge Ingstad 103

J

Constable Samuel Jeffers 142
Andy Jones 61
Cathy Jones 61

K

James Kavanagh 137
RCMP Constable David Keith 142
Joanne Kelly 56

L

Walter Learning 66
Edward Low 111

M

Linden MacIntyre 65
Dr. Cluny MacPherson 133
Henry Mainwaring 111
Shaun Majumder 60
Greg Malone 63
Mary March 98
Guglielmo Marconi 24, 117, 121, 146
James Foster McCoubrey 73
Rick Mercer 60
Constable William Moss 142
John Munn 26
Rex Murphy 68

N

Sheila NaGiera 34, 75
Gary Noseworthy 142
John Nutt 111

O

Seamus O'Regan 63
Mary Ewing Outerbridge 96

P

Florence Paterson 61
Peter Penashue 164
John Philpot 135
Gordon Pinsent 58, 59
Eleanor Power 137

R

John Reeves 135
Michael Ricketts 66
Bartholomew Roberts 110
Captain Mark Rudkin 135
Michael Ryder 131

S

Lawyer Louise Saunders 144
Tommy Sexton 63
Joseph R. (Joey) Smallwood 68, 160
Catherine Mandeville Snow 138
Sebastian Spence 57
Herbert Spratt 140
Lady Helena E. Squires 76
Constable Francis P. Stamp 141
Kim Stockwood 69, 70
John J. Sullivan 144
Calvin Augustus Swyers 142

T

Greg Thomey 63
Joseph V. Tremblett 142
Shannon Tweed 56
Governor General Lord Tweedsmuir 26

W

Nick Wall 69
Mary Walsh 61
Governor Sir Humphrey Walwyn 26
Michael Whelan 137
Judge Harry Winter 26

Y

John Young 142